Dictionary of
British Kings
and Queens

BROCKHAMPTON PRESS
LONDON

This edition published 1995 by Brockhampton Press, a
member of the Hodder Headline PLC Group.

ISBN 1 86019 073 1

Printed and bound in Slovenia

CONTENTS

INTRODUCTION

Roman Britain

The British islands first became known to the Romans through Caesar's two expeditions in 55 and 54 BC. The main island was generally known by them as *Brittania*, but it was not until the time of Claudius, nearly a hundred years after, that the Romans made a serious attempt to convert Britain into a Roman province. There is evidence to suggest that there were tribal rulers in Britain as early as 4500 years ago, but the contemporary records of the Romans invaders give the first clear proof that there were Iron Age tribal kings and queens. The tribes they encountered were migrants from mainland Europe who spoke Celtic tongues akin to Gaelic, Irish and Welsh and used coins similar to those used in Greece and Rome. Among the larger of these tribes were the Atrebates (based around Sussex), Brigantes (founded York as their capital), Catuvellauni (based around Hertfordshire), Regni (based in Sussex) and the Iceni (based around Norfolk and Suffolk). Some of the leaders of these tribes became 'client' rulers under Rome and retained much of their power.

The heart of Roman rule was in the south east of England but Roman armies also came into contact with the tribes of the north. The battle at 'Mons Graupius', thought to have been in Aberdeenshire, gave the Romans a temporary foothold; but the rugged terrain, as much as the resistance of the tribes, meant they had to retire behind the wall, completed in AD 120 by Hadrian, between the Solway and the Tyne. Thus the southern part of the island alone remained Roman, and became specially known as 'Britannia', while the northern portion was distinctively called 'Caledonia'.

Eight Roman Emperors were proclaimed in Britannia and it became an important part of the Empire, but by 400 BC attacks from northern Europe, Scotland and Ireland had almost exhausted the resources of the province. Hadrian's Wall was abandoned and troops withdrawn from important outposts until, around 415 BC, the formal rule of the Romans ended.

Early English Kings

After the Romans withdrew from southern Britain, the tribal rulers were left to defend their territories against increasingly frequent attacks from fierce northern tribesmen. They also had to contend with the invasions of Germanic tribes eager to drive them out and settle new lands. From what are now called the Netherlands, Germany, Denmark and France came the Angles, Saxons and Jutes to set up hundreds of petty states.

In time the larger of these states swallowed the smaller until, around 700, there were about forty established statelets. Eventually a group of the seven most prominent states emerged, generally referred to as the *Heptarchy*, which dominated most of the southern part of Britain. This consisted of the kingdoms of Kent, the South Saxons (in Surrey and Sussex), the East Angles (East Anglia), the East Saxons (Essex and Middlesex), the West Saxons or Wessex (Devon, Dorset, Somerset and part of Cornwall), Northumbria (Northumberland, York and Durham and also south east Scotland), and the Kingdom of Mercia (which included Gloucester, Leicester and Chester). To the north were the Picts and Scots, to the west were the Celts of Wales. The Britons fleeing the European invaders had settled in Strathclyde (the south west of Scotland) and Cornwall. All Anglo-Saxon kings (except those of Essex) claimed the war god Woden as their ancestor, and with the approval of a council of advisers, known as the *Witan*, bequeathed their crown to a son. At times one king became *Bretwalda*, or overlord, of all the rest. The battle for supremacy between these seven kingdoms persisted until at length Wessex overran Mercia, Sussex and all the lands south of the Humber, and the whole came to be known as Angle-land, or England.

These were uncertain times however, and the Angle kings were frequently defeated by the ambitions of Danish invaders. Their advance was checked for a time by Alfred the Great (who also ensured that those he defeated were converted to Christianity) and many were diverted to northern France where their settlements became Normandy. Alfred was the first to bring about some form of national unity among the Anglo-Saxons, but his descendants could not claim to rule all England, and fought again against the Danes, with varying degrees of success, to maintain power. By 1016 England had again been made to submit to foreign rule as the Danish king, Canute, made England part of a greater northern European empire. When this empire finally collapsed England was left disunited; a state of affairs which was finally exploited by a Norman, Duke William of Normandy, who began his conquest by defeating the English forces at Hastings in 1066.

Picts and Scots

The inhabitants of the northern lands, known to the Romans as Caledonians and to the Britons as the people of Albion, could be distinguished into Goidels (or Gaels) and Picts. The Gaels were of a similar stock to the British, and, since the eighteenth century, British and Gaels have alike been termed 'Celtic'. This usage originated in the discovery of an affinity between the language of Brittany and those of the Welsh and of the Scottish Highlanders. It is, however, important to make a distinction between the Brythonic Celts of Wales, Cumbria, and Strathclyde, and the Goidelic Celts or Gaels of the Northern Highlands. By the sixth century these northern tribes were more commonly known as Picts, which means literally 'painted people'.

As well as the Picts, a body of Celts from Ireland, known as Scots, had, by the middle of the sixth century, settled in what is the present day county of Argyll and founded the kingdom of Dalriada. This kingdom consisted of Argyll, part of Northern Ireland and the islands of the Inner Hebrides.

The amalgamation of the Scots, Picts, Britons and Angles into one kingdom was a slow and lengthy process. The foundation for the ultimate union of the Scots and the Picts was laid by St Columba who travelled to the already christianised kingdom of Dalriada in 563. The actual occasion of the union of Scots and Picts, however, was to come via a combination of factors. Dynastic inter-marriage, religious unity and Scandanavian aggression all played their part, but it was the strong leadership of Kenneth mac-Alpin, king of Scots, which finally brought the kingdoms together. Under his guidance the Scots became the dominant force in the land and the idea of the Picts as an independent people largely died out.

The amalgamation of the Lothians and of Strathclyde with *Alba* (the kingdom of Picts and Scots) was delayed for two centuries. Strathclyde was finally merged through dynastic inheritance, but it took the collapse of Nothumbrian power and the consolidation of England under the successors of Alfred the Great to unite the Scots and Angles. Successive monarchs of Alba tried to add Lothian to their dominions, but it was not until 1018 that it was finally annexed and the whole of the historical kingdom of Scotland was ruled by one king, who maintained the title of 'King of Scots'.

Early Welsh Kings

Previous to the Roman occupation, Wales appears to have been chiefly inhabited by three British tribes, called the Silures, Dimaetae, and Ordivices. During the latter period of the Roman occupation the subject part of the island was divided into four provinces, of which one, including the country from the Dee to the Severn, was called *Brittannia Secunda*. It was after the invasion of the Saxons that the country acquired a distinctive national character as the refuge of the vanquished Britons who were gradually driven to the west. From this period until the final conquest of the country by Edward I there is little but a succession of petty wars between the rival chiefs or kings into which both countries during a great part of the Saxon period were divided, or the more systematic efforts of the larger monarchy to absorb the smaller. By war and marriage three main territories were established: Gwynedd in North Wales; Powys in the central region; and Deheubarth in South Wales. Of the three, Gwynedd spread its influence the furthest, and sometimes dominated all Wales. By 1200, however, Welsh kings had been reduced to lords and princes owing homage to the King of England. The last of the Welsh princes, Llywelyn, who revolted against Edward I, was defeated by the Earl of Mortimer in 1284. Since that time the principality has been incorporated with England and Wales has given the title of Prince of Wales to the heir-apparent of the British Crown.

Early Irish Kings

As in Western Europe generally, the earliest inhabitants of Ireland are believed to have been of Iberian race, and therefore akin to the modern Basques. They were followed by the Celts, different tribes of whom probably arrived at different times. Among these the Scots were the latest, and subsequently got the upper hand, so that their name became generally applied to all the inhabitants. The land was divided into five principal kingdoms—Ulster, Munster, Leinster, Connaught, and Meath—which were each divided in turn into lesser divisions or chiefdoms. Each king or chieftan desired to become the *Ard-Ri* (high king) of the whole island but for centuries no one achieved any real degree of supremacy.

Following the introduction of Christianity and Christian literature by St Patrick, Ireland became an important seat of Western learning. Its internal condition, however, was far from satisfactory. Divided among a number of hostile kings or chiefs, it had been long torn by internal wars, and for nearly two centuries ravaged by the Danes, numbers of whom settled in the country, when, in the beginning of the eleventh century, Brian Boru united the greater part of the island under his sceptre and subdued the northern invaders. After the death of Brian the island relapsed into its former state of division and anarchy. In this state of matters Henry II of England obtained a Papal Bull giving him the right to subdue it. In 1172 Henry entered Ireland himself, and partly through the favour of the clergy, the great princes did homage to him and acknowledged his supremacy. Many Norman barons and their followers now settled in the country, but the English power was far from being established over it. For long only a part was recognized as English territory (generally known as 'the Pale'), and this was governed by various nobles, subject to a Viceroy. The greater part of the island remained unconquered and English supremacy was threatened frequently by rebellions of Irish chiefs and barons. It was not until the reign of Henry VIII that the title of King, instead of Lord, of Ireland was properly established. The chieftains of Ulster remained fiercely independent however, and continued to seek allies on the continent to rid Ireland of the English. During the reign of Elizabeth I they were eventually forced to flee and this 'Flight of the Earls' became a turning point in the history of England's involvement in Ireland for it was then that the 'Plantation'—the settlement of English and Scottish Protestants in Ulster—began.

Ireland remained under English, and then British, kings and queens until the time of Edward VIII's abdication in 1936. Independence was finally achieved in this year when the Irish Free State abolished the monarchy and formally became a republic. British monarchs continue to reign over Northern Ireland, comprising most of what had been the ancient kingdom of Ulster.

A

Aed (d.878) King of Scots. Reigned in 878. The son of KENNETH MAC-ALPIN, he succeeded his brother CONSTANTINE I as king but reigned for less than a year. He was reputedly murdered by his first cousin, GIRIC, the son of DONALD I, a rival for the throne.

Aed Find (d.*c.*778) King of Scots. Reigned from 768 to 778. He invaded the Pictish heartland early in his reign but the results of his efforts are not known.

Aed Finnliath (d.*c.*879) High king of Ireland. Reigned from 862 to 868. In 861 he joined with a Norse force against the ruling high king, MAEL SECHNAILL. On his death a year later Aed became high king and turned against his former allies. Over the next five years of his reign he was greatly troubled by inroads made by the Vikings but won an important battle against them at Killineery in 868.

Aelfwald (d.749) King of East Anglia. Reigned from 713 to 749. An under-king of Mercia under the powerful ETHELBALD from 740.

Aelle (d.588) King of Deira. Reigned from *c.*560 to 588. A son of IDA, he was the first king of this small kingdom (roughly Humberside) to establish independence from Bernicia (roughly Northumberland). On his death the kingdom was taken by his brother, ETHELRIC (who ruled Bernicia after his father), and his two sons fled the kingdom. Ethelric became the first king of Northumbria.

Aelle (d.867) King of Northumbria. Reigned from 866 to 867. He was chosen to be king following the removal of the unpopular OSBERT. Soon after a large Norse army, which had invaded in 865, took advantage of the royal in-fighting to seize York, the chief city of Northumbria. After resolving their dispute, Osbert and Aelle mounted a joint attack in 867. They were at first successful, but at length lost their army in a climactic battle. Osbert was killed in the fighting but Aelle was sacrificed to the Norse war god Odin in a gruesome ritual. The leader of the Norsemen, Ivar the Boneless, justified the killing by falsely claiming that Aelle had slain his father by throwing him into a pit of vipers.

Aelle (d.*c.*514) King of Sussex. According to the *Anglo-Saxon Chronicle* he established the South Saxon kingdom after landing around 477 and defeating a force of Britons at a place called Cymenesora. With his third son CISSA he besieged an old Roman fort at Pevensay held by Britons in 491 and massacred the occupants. He came to be regarded as *Bretwalda*, or overlord among the Anglo-Saxon kings of southern England although at this time the success of the invaders was not certain and the title was little more than honorary.

Aesc (d.512) King of Kent. Reigned from 488 to 512. Son of HENGEST and nephew of HORSA, the first Jutish kings of Kent. He succeeded to the kingdom on the death of his father and soon established himself as a powerful ruler. Many of his battles against the Welsh and the men of Kent are recorded in the *Anglo-Saxon Chronicle*. Although his father and uncle are regarded as the first kings, Aesc, also given as 'Oisc', provided the dynastic name of 'Oiscingas'.

Aescwine King of Essex. Reigned from *c*.527 to *c*.587. Thought to have been the founder of the small kingdom of East Saxons which, with London as its capital, was later absorbed by Wessex.

Aescwine King of Wessex. Reigned from 674 to 676. The son of CENFUS and a descendant of King COEL.

Aiden (d.606) King of Scots. Reigned from *c*.575 to 606. Ordained at Dunadd by his cousin Colum Cille (St Columba) in what was probably the first Christian coronation in Britain, Aiden was a descendant of FERGUS MOR and did much to consolidate the kingdom of Dalriada. Influenced by St Columba, he sought an alliance with the king of the O'Neill dynasty in Ulster to protect the monastic community founded by St Columba on the small island of Iona. This was acheived at Druim Cett soon after Aiden's coronation. Sometime between 580 and 585 he captured the Orkneys and Isle of Man respectively, thus extending his kingdom. During his reign he fought many battles against the Picts, Britons and Angles but was finally defeated in 603 by ETHELFRITH at Degsastan, near Liddesdale. As Aiden lost most of his army and a son in the battle the Northumbrian ruler was free to advance further north and west. At his death he was over seventy years old and was succeeded by his son EOCHAID.

Alchred King of Northumbria. Reigned from 765 to 774. He is known to have been a supporter of missions to Europe and was in contact with the Frankish king Charlemagne. Deposed in favour of ETHELRED, he sought shelter among the Picts.

Aldfrith (d.705) King of Northumbria. Reigned from 685 to 705. The son of Oswy's mistress, Aldfrith combined statesman-like qualities with a reputation as a man of letters. In his pursuit of learning it is said he exchanged an estate in return for a book which had been brought by a monk from Rome. He was succeeded by his eight year-old son, OSRED.

Aldwulf King of East Anglia. Reigned from 663 to 713. Son of ETHELHERE and a Northumbrian princess, Hereswith of Deira.

Aldwulf King of Sussex. He reigned briefly c.765 and is known to have made a land grant to the Church.

Alexander I (the Fierce) (1077-1124) King of Scots. Reigned from 1107 to 1124. The fifth son of MALCOLM III (Canmore), the first king of all Scot-

and Margaret of England, he was born at Dumbarton and succeeded his elder brother EDGAR as king. He ruled only that part of the kingdom to the north of the Forth and Clyde as the south (Cumbria, Strathclyde and southern Lothian) had been bequeathed to David, Edgar's younger brother, for him to govern as Earl. As a devout patron of the church did much to strengthen the religious independence of his kingdom. He revived the see at Dunkeld, established the Augustinian priory at Scone and the abbey on the island of Inchcolm. During his reign many new castles were also built, including a new royal castle at Stirling.

He maintained good relations with HENRY I and encouraged Norman settlement in lowland Scotland where they began to introduce feudalism as a system for holding land and built castles in the Norman style. He also took an active part in Henry's campaign against the rebellious Welsh kings in 1114 and married Sybilla, his illegitimate daughter. The marriage produced no legitimate offspring, although descendents of his natural son, Malcolm Mac-Heth, later made unsuccessful claims to parts of Caithness. He was succeeded by his younger brother DAVID I upon his death at Stirling. He was interred at Dunfermline's Abbey Church.

Significant events of Alexander I's reign

- 1112 – Berwick-upon-Tweed becomes the first royal burgh in Scotland.

- 1114 – With Alexander's help Henry I receives oaths of obedience from Welsh kings.

Alexander II (1198-1249) King of Scots. Reigned
from 1214 to 1249. The son of WILLIAM I, 'the Lion',
and Ermengarde de Beaumont, he was born at
Haddington and succeeded his father at the age of
sixteen. His accession was immediately disputed and
an army was gathered by Donald mac-William, a rival to the throne. They soon landed from Ireland but
were defeated by the Earl of Mar who ordered the
execution of the leaders.

During Alexander's reign there was no serious
conflict with England and he was married to King
JOHN's eldest daughter, Princess Joan in 1221 but the
relationship was far from stable. As the young Scottish king had red hair, John boasted of how he would
'hunt the red fox cub from his lair', but John was being forced by his barons to sign the Magna Carta and
Alexander stood firmly with them. Following a successful campaign in the north of England the barons
paid homage to Alexander, but following King
John's death the barons broke the agreements made
with Alexander and he raised an army against them.
Alexander was unsuccessful and, constrained to
come to terms with England, had to do homage to the
new king, HENRY III. He was an able politician however, and gave up his claims to Northumberland,
Westmoreland and Cumberland in order to agree the
peace. This led to the Treaty of York of 1237 which
fixed the borders between the two countries roughly
where they are today and Alexander received estates
in northern England worth £200 a year. It was an un-
easy peace however, and it was seven years until the

relationship improved with the betrothal of Henry's three year-old daughter, Margaret, to Alexander's son and heir

He was an intelligent and energetic monarch; as well as being a good soldier he governed wisely and introduced measures to modernize the administration of his kingdom. As a devoted patron of the church he was responsible for the founding of several important monasteries and abbeys. Despite these progressive achievements he was still very much a king of his times; this was demonstrated by his punishment of those present at the brutal murder of Bishop Adam of Caithness when he ordered that the hands and feet of eighty men be cut off.

He died after falling ill with a fever at Kerrera, an island opposite Oban, whilst on route to join his naval fleet for an expedition in which he hoped to wrest the Hebrides from King Haakron IV of Norway. Princess Joan died childless in 1238; Alexander's second wife, Marie de Coucy, daughter of Baron de Coucy of Picardy, provided his successor, ALEXANDER III. He is buried at Melrose Abbey.

Significant events of Alexander II's reign

- 1215 – Alexander receives homage of the
  northern English barons.
- 1216 – King John dies. Henry III
  becomes king.
- 1221 – Alexander marries Henry's sister, Joan.
- 1237 – Treaty of York fixes Scottish border
  with England.

Alexander III (1241-1286) King of Scots. Reigned
from 1249 to 1286. The only son of ALEXANDER II and
Marie de Coucy succeeded his father when still only
eight years of age. He married Princess Margaret,
eldest daughter of HENRY III of England, to whom he
had been betrothed, two years later. Rival court factions jostled for positions during his minority and
rebel lords, led by the Comyns of Monteith and
Buchan, attempted to take control of the government
when Alexander was sixteen by holding the king hostage. This angered Henry III of England who offered
to keep an army in northern England until the difficulty was resolved. Negotiations at Jedburgh finally
settled the matter and the Comyns were reconciled to
their rivals in government and to the English king.
Later the same year a council of ten people were chosen to care for Alexander until he reached his majority in 1262 and the dispute between Henry, the
Comyns and the Scottish government was formally
ended.

It was not long after assuming full powers that
Alexander began to assert his position as king. Like
his father, he was eager to bring the Hebrides under
his sway, and this he was able to accomplish in a few
years after defeating an invasion force led by the
Norse king Haakon at Largs. He bought the Isle of
Man and the Hebrides from Norway's Magnus VI for
£2666 and in 1266 signed the Treaty of Perth which
established his control over all the Western Isles.
This brought to an end nearly four centuries of Norse
domination of the Hebrides. For the first time the

mainland and islands of Scotland had been brought together under one sovereign, although Orkney and Shetland still belonged to Norway.

Alexander was strenuous in asserting the independence both of his kingdom and of the Scottish Church, but his relationship with England remained peaceful. At his wedding, when he was only ten years old, he is said to have nearly been tricked into doing homage to Henry but had the presence of mind to evade Henry's approaches. The king of England never gave up however, and continued to appeal to Alexander. Following Henry's death he attended EDWARD I's coronation only after receiving written confirmation that the independence of the kingdom of Scotland would not be compromised. For the rest of his reign he managed to keep on good terms with his neighbour, despite refusing to do homage except for those lands he held in the north of England.

Alexander main difficulty was in securing a successor. His wife's death in 1275 was followed by that of his two sons, David and Alexander, both childless. In order to secure the succession he married Yolande of Dreaux; but less than six months later, while riding in the dark along the cliffs between Edinburgh and Kinghorn in Fife to meet his wife, his horse stumbled and threw him. The body of the last Celtic king was found at the foot of the cliffs the next morning. The marriage of his daughter Margaret to Eric II of Norway had brought a daughter however, and this infant, MARGARET, the Maid of Norway had been recognised as heir to the throne by Parliament two years before. She was proclaimed as Queen of Scotland, despite the unpopularity of female succession, but died on the sea-crossing from Norway and never put a foot on Scottish soil.

Significant events of Alexander III's reign

- 1263 – Alexander defeats Norse invaders at the Battle of Largs.

- 1266 – Alexander gains control of the Hebrides under the Treaty of Perth.

- 1274 – Alexander attends coronation of Edward I of England.

- 1285 – Margaret, the Maid of Norway, is recognized as heir presumptive.

Alfred the Great (849-901) King of Wessex. Reigned from 871 to 901. Alfred was born at Wantage in Berkshire, his father being ETHELWULF, son of EGBERT, king of the West Saxons. He succeeded his brother ETHELRED in 871, at a time when the Danes, or Norsemen, had extended their conquests widely over the country; they had completely overrun the Kingdom of the West Saxons (or Wessex) by 878. Alfred, the king of Wessex, was obliged to flee in disguise. At length he gathered a small force and having fortified himself on the Isle of Athelney, formed by the confluence of the Rivers Parret and Tone amid the marshes of Somerset, he was able to make frequent raids on the enemy. It was during his time here that he, according to legend, disguised himself as a harper and entered into the camp of King GUTHRUM. Having ascertained that the Danes felt themselves secure,

he returned to his troops and led them against the enemy. He gained such a decided victory that fourteen
days afterwards the Danes begged for peace. This
battle took place in May, 878, near Edington in Wiltshire. Later he took London and repulsed a Danish
seaborne invasion. Alfred allowed the Danes who
were already in the country to remain, on condition
that they gave hostages, took a solemn oath to quit
Essex, and embraced Christianity. Under these terms,
known as the Peace of Wedmere their king, Guthrum,
was baptized, together with thirty of his followers. In
return they received that portion of the east of England now occupied by the counties of Norfolk, Suffolk, and Cambridge, as a place of residence. By this
time all outside of Danish-ruled England also recognized Alfred as king of all England.

The few years of tranquillity (886–93) which followed were employed by Alfred in rebuilding the
towns that had suffered most during the war, particularly London. He consolidated his power by raising
around thirty forts, including Oxford and Hastings.
He also set about training his people in arms and in
agriculture; in improving the navy; in systematizing
the laws and internal administration; and in literary
labours and the advancement of learning. He re-established the monasteries (as a youth he had twice
visited the Pope in Rome and had been devoutly
Christian since) and schools sacked by the Danes and
caused many manuscripts to be translated from
Latin; he himself translated several works into
Anglo-Saxon, such as the Psalms, *Æsop's Fables*,

Boethius on the *Consolation of Philosophy*, the *History of Orosius* and Bede's *Ecclesiastical History*. He also drew up several original works in Anglo-Saxon and initiated the translation of Latin records to form the *Anglo-Saxon Chronicle*.

These labours were interrupted, about 894, by an invasion of the Norsemen, who, after a struggle of three years in which they tried to settle lands in the south of England, were finally driven out. Alfred died in 901 and is buried at Winchester. He had married, in 868, Alswith, the daughter of a Mercian nobleman, and left three daughters and two sons, Edward, who succeeded him, and Ethelward, who died in 922. Their descendants ruled England until 1066.

Alpin (d.*c*.840) King of Scots. Reigned from *c*.837 to *c*.840. This semi-legendary king ruled Dalriada for only a short period before being killed by an unknown assailant. He was the 34th king of Dalriada and is thought to be the son of EOCHAID 'the Venomous' perhaps by a Pictish mother, and the father of KENNETH MAC-ALPIN and DONALD I.

Alric King of Kent. Reigned from 747 to 762. Succeeded his brother EADBERT I as joint ruler with his other brother, ETHELBERT II.

Anarawd King of Gwynedd. Reigned from 878 to 916. The son of RHODI MAWR, he shared with his five brothers the rule of lands won by his father. In 885 he made an alliance with the Norse king of Dublin against the other kings of Wales who were them-

selves allied with King ALFRED of Wessex. This made
him the most powerful ruler in Wales and the alliance
held for eight years before he finally made peace
with Alfred.

Androco (*fl*.AD 20) High king of the British tribes. Son
of CASWALLON, he ruled the Catuvellauni tribe based
around Hertfordshire and followed his father as the
high king of the various tribes he had united against
the Romans.

Anna (d.654) King of East Anglia. Reigned from *c*.633
to 654. A devout Christian son of INE who produced
four daughters known for their piety. He was killed in
battle fighting PENDA of Mercia.

Anne (1665-1714) Queen of England and later Great
Britain and Ireland. Reigned from 1702 to 1714. The
second daughter of JAMES II, then Duke of York, and
Anne Hyde, daughter of the Earl of Clarendon. With
her father's permisson she was educated according to
the principles of the English Church. In 1683 she was
married to Prince George, son of King Ferdinand III
of Denmark and brother of King Christian V of Denmark. On the arrival of the Prince of Orange in 1688,
Anne wished to remain with her father; but she was
prevailed upon by Lord Churchill (afterwards Duke
of Marlborough) and his wife to join the triumphant
party. After the death of WILLIAM III she ascended the
English throne and was coronated at Westminster
Abbey.

    Her character was essentially weak, and she re-
mained distant from the new political parties called

the Whigs and the Tories, although she presided over meetings of the Cabinet. Most of the principal events of her reign are connected with the war of the Spanish Succession. The eighteenth century had opened with a series of events in Europe which made war inevitable as it was essential for England to have an Austrian, instead of a French prince, ascend the Spanish throne. The commander of the English army, The Duke of Marlborough was a brilliant soldier, arguably the best ever produced by England, and he soon routed a combined French and Bavarian army at Blenheim. The Queen rewarded her commander with the estate on which was built Blenheim Palace. Two years later Marlborough drove the French from the Netherlands following the victory af Ramillies and King Louis sued for peace. Instead of negotiating a Treaty with the French however, England negotiated an Act of Union with Scotland. In May 1707 the two Parliaments of Scotland and England, not without some difficulty, were finally united. The united kingdoms came to be called Great Britain and had as its symbolic flag the Union Jack.

Meanwhile the war with the French was vigorously prosecuted; the British forces defeated the French at Oudenarde and continued to seize valuable French colonies elsewhere. At home however, there were disputes within the Government as the Tories, who had never been in favour of the government funding wars which served the financial interests of the Whigs, took control of the Commons. Anne then fell out with her old friend, the Duchess of Marlborough,

and came under the influence of the Tories.
Marlborough was soon recalled from Europe and the
Treaty of Utrecht negotiated with the French. Austria
was to have the Spanish Netherlands, the crowns of
Spain and France were to be united, and Britain was
to retain the valuable colonies of Gibraltar, Nova
Scotia, Newfoundland and Minorca.

England was still divided however, as Anne
wanted to secure the succession to her brother James
against the wishes of the cabinet. The Act of Settlement eventually assigned the crown to JAMES I's Protestant descendants of the House of Hanover if Anne
were to die childless. Grieved at the disappointment
of her wishes, she fell into a state of weakness and
lethargy, and died. She was to be the last of the Stuart
monarchs.

The reign of Anne was distinguished not only by
the brilliant successes of the British arms, but also on
account of the number of admirable and excellent
writers who flourished at this time, among whom
were Pope, Swift, and Addison. Anne bore her husband many children, all of whom died in infancy, except one son, the Duke of Gloucester, who died at the
age of twelve.

Significant events of Anne's reign

- 1702 – The War of the Spanish Succession
  commences.

  The first daily newspaper, *The Daily
  Courant*, is printed in London.

- 1704 – The Battle of Blenheim.

- 1704 – Gilbraltar is taken from Spain by
  Sir George Rook.
- 1705 – Barcelona is taken by the Earl of
  Peterborough.
- 1706 – The Battle of Ramillies.
- 1707 – The Act of Union creates Great Britain.
- 1708 – The Battle of Oudenarde.

  Prince George of Denmark dies.

  Minorca falls to the English troops.
- 1709 – The Battle of Malplaquet.
- 1710 – Tory administration takes power.
- 1711 – Marborough is relieved of his post.
- 1713 – The War of the Spanish Succession is
  ended by the Treaty of Utrecht.

  For the last time in England a death
  sentence for witchcraft is carried out.
- 1714 – Sophia of Hanover dies, her son George
  becomes heir to England's throne.

Artgal (d.871) King of Strathclyde. His kingdom was
subject to raids from Norse invaders and in 870 they
sacked Dumbarton, an important stronghold on the
Dublin to York trade route. He escaped capture but
was later put to death on the orders of CONSTANTINE I.

Arthur (*fl.*500) British tribal king. A figure best
known from popular legend who may have been
based on the tribal king who led the Britons to victory at Mount Badon (518) as chronicled by Nennius
in *Historia Britonium* (9th century). Another writer,

Gildan, a contemporary of Nennius, dates this battle at around 500 and does not connect it with the figure of Arthur. The legends of King Arthur appear in Welsh literature of the 10th century and also feature in Geoffrey Monmouth's *History of the Kings of Britain* in the 12th century. Later writers contributed to the tales; most famously Sir Thomas Mallory, who translated from the French Arthurian romance, *Le Morte d'Arthur*.

B

Balliol, **Edward** (1287-1364) King of Scots. Reigned from 1332 to 1341. The son of JOHN BALLIOL, he was held prisoner in Normandy and England after his father's abdication. When ROBERT I of Scotland died, leaving his young son David as heir, Balliol became EDWARD III's candidate for the throne, although he was also acknowledged by many Scots as the heir. Soon after the coronation of DAVID II he landed a considerable army at Kinghorn in Fife and with the support of dispossesed English and Scottish nobles and many mercenary soldiers, he defeated the Earl of Mar's army at Dupplin Moor. David II fled to France where he was to remain until he was seventeen. Balliol was eventually crowned at Scone in 1332 and, as he accepted Edward III as overlord of his kingdom, put Scotland in the control of England. This proved unacceptable to a great many Scots lords and he had to flee to Carlisle where he survived as a powerless king during the minority of David II. His enthonement had nonetheless entailed the surrender of much of lowland Scotland to England and the country was thrown into civil war with rival factions of nobles contesting estates. An army led by Scots lords attempting to end the siege of Berwick was subsequently defeated by an English army at Halidon Hill in 1333. Edward's army advanced again in 1334 and after taking Roxburgh, forced the Scots lords to accept Balliol as their king. He had no real power but remained a puppet of the English king until David II returned from France. Balliol was eventually dismissed with a pension by Edward III in 1356 and died on his family estate (Bailleul) in Picardy, France, in 1364.

Significant events of Edward Balliol's reign

- 1332 – Battle of Dupplin Moor. Balliol is crowned at Scone.
- 1333 – Edward III invades and defeats Scots at Halidon Hill.
- 1334 – Balliol accepted as king by Scots lords.
- 1337 – The Hundred Years' War begins.
- 1341 – Edinburgh Castle regained from the English.
- 1342 – David II regains the throne of Scotland.

Balliol, John (1249-1313) King of Scots. Reigned from 1292 to 1296. The son of Devorguilla Balliol, John married the daughter of the Earl of Surrey and owned vast estates in both England and Scotland. His claim to the throne in 1291 was contested by a dozen rivals (known as the Competitors), including Robert Bruce of Annadale, the grandfather of ROBERT I. The Guardians of Scotland, fearing a civil war, asked EDWARD I of England to intervene. Edward I took advantage of the situation and demanded allegiance and custody of several important castles before deciding on Balliol. Edward continued to make demands of the Scots and his interventions soon became intolerable. After demanding Scots troops for a war with France the Community of the Realm persuaded Balliol to renounce his allegiance. The auld alliance with France was renewed in 1295 and Edward invaded Scotland in retaliation. Following his defeat at Dunbar, John sued for peace and surrendered at Stracathro in July 1296. He was forced to relinquish the crown and the English forces which overran Scotland took away or burned many records and removed the Stone of Destiny (the Coronation Stone of Scone) to Westminster Abbey. Imprisoned in the Tower of London, Balliol was later given Bailleul, his ancestral home in France, where he died in 1313. His son, EDWARD BALLIOL, later renewed the claim to Scotland's throne with the support of England.

Significant events of John Balliol's reign

- 1295 – Franco-Scottish treaty begins the Auld Alliance
- 1296 – Balliol is deposed.

  Edward I invades Scotland.

Bealdred King of Kent. Reigned from 807 to 825. Ruled as an under-king of Mercia under the control of Cuthred's brother, King COENWULF. He was driven out in 825 by EGBERT of Wessex who soon after became overlord of the East Angles as well as Kent, Surrey, Sussex and Essex.

Beli (d.722) King of Strathclyde. He successfully defended his kingdom from attacks by OENGUS, king of the Picts. His son and successor, TEWDWR, later won an important battle against the Picts at Mugdock, near Glasgow in 750.

Beonna King of East Anglia. Reigned *c.*760. Known to have issued a coinage during his reign.

Beonred King of Mercia. Reigned in 757. The successor to the throne of King ETHELBALD of Mercia, he was challenged by OFFA, a cousin of the former king. Disorder followed and the confederacy of kingdoms which had been built by Ethelbald was weakened as the two rivals fought. It was only a matter of months before Offa deposed him.

Beorhtwulf (d.853) King of Mercia. Reigned from 840 to 853. He succeeded WIGLAF as king and endured a period of sustained Viking attacks. He was finally routed in 852 when over 350 ships stormed London and Canterbury and he died a year later. He was succeeded by his son Burgred.

Beornwulf (d.827) King of Mercia. Reigned from 823 to 827. He deposed CEOLWULF in 823 and soon after led an army into Wessex. After some initial success he was defeated by EGBERT and later killed near Swindon. He was succeeded by LUDECA, previously an ealdorman.

Beortric (d.802) King of Wessex. Reigned from 757 to 802. He married Eadburga of Mercia, a daughter of OFFA, and was succeeded by EGBERT.

Berhtun (d.686) King of Sussex. Reigned 686. Ruling for less than a year, he was killed during an invasion of Kent.

Boadicea (or **Boudicca**) (d.61) Queen of the Iceni tribe. Wife of PRASUTAGUS, a client of Rome, whose lands in Norfolk and Suffolk were taken by the Romans after his death. Homes and estates were burned and plundered, Boudicca was flogged and her daughters raped. In retaliation she gathered a large army and led a violent rebellion which took London, St Albans and Colchester while the Roman governor Paulinius was in Wales. When Polonius returned he violently suppressed the rebellion and the defeated Boadicea killed herself with poison.

Bred (d.842) King of Picts. Reigned in 842. He ascended the throne on the death of his father, UURAD, but his reign did not last the year as he was deposed by his brother, KINETH.

Brian Boru (c.941-1014) High king of Ireland. Reigned from 1002 to 1014. The king of Munster from 976. He took the title of High king after defeating his great rival MAEL SECHNAILL II, the last of the O'Neill kings, at Athlone. After extending his kingdom to take in much of southern Ireland, he put an end to Norse ambitions in Ireland by his victory at the Battle of Clontarf (1014) near Dublin. The losses suffered in this conflict were great and in the confusion Brian Boru was killed in his tent by defeated and fleeing Danes. Mael Sechnaill II quickly reclaimed the title of high king but after his death in 1024 no king was able to secure the position for any notable period of time for over 150 years. This effectively ended royal rule in Ireland.

As well as a soldier Brian Boru was a patron of education and religion. He established monasteries and encouraged the preservation of the old Irish sagas as well as the writing of poetry and prose. Three O'Brien descendents remained kings of Munster until the next century (1119). Their main kingdom disappeared in 1194, but the O'Briens remained kings of north Munster until 1543. The kingdom then became an earldom under HENRY VII. It remained an earldom until 1741 when the 8th earl died childless.

Bridei I (d.586) King of Picts. Reigned from 556 to 586. His royal court at Inverness was visited by St Columba but he did not convert to Christianity.

Bridei II (d.641) King of Picts. Reigned from 635 to 641. A brother of GARNARD.

Bridei III (d.692) King of Picts. Reigned from 671 to 692. The son of DREST I's sister. He was the first of the Pictish kings to be recognized overlord of all Pictland after defeating King EGFRITH of Northumbria in the battle of Nectansmere in 685. Egfrith had installed his cousin Drest as ruler of the Picts in order to consolidate his power in the north.

Bridei IV (d.706) King of Picts. Reigned from 696 to 706. The son of DREST's sister.

Bridei V (d.763) King of Picts. Reigned from 761 to 763. The brother of OENGUS.

Brude (d.845) King of Picts. Reigned from 843 to 845. The son of Uurad's sister, he ascended the throne after killing his uncle Kineth. He was converted to Christianity by St Columba.

Bruce, Edward (1276-1318) High king of Ireland. Reigned from 1315 to 1318. One of the five sons of Robert, the Earl of Carrick and Marjorie, Countess of Carrick, and the younger brother of Robert I of Scotland (his three other brothers were executed following Robert's defeats at Methven and Dalry). A fearless commander, he aided his brother during his guerilla-style campaign of raids on English held castles. By mid-1308 Edward had overrun Galloway, while his brother had control of much of the north. He failed in his attempt to take Stirling in 1313 and made a truce with Philip de Mowbray which made Bannockburn inevitable.

Invited to Ireland, where he had grown up, in 1315 by the king of Tyrone he led an army in a difficult campaign for a year before being crowned High king of Ireland. His tactic of destroying everything in his path as he progressed through Ireland made him an unpopular figure. He failed to take Dublin despite assistance from his brother and was killed at Dundalk in 1318 along with many of his supporters. He married Isabell of Atholl before Dundalk and had two sons.

Burgred King of Mercia. Reigned from 853 to 874. The son of Beorhtwulf, he married Ethelswith, daughter of Ethelwulf of Wessex, and with the assistance of the latter frequently raided north Wales. He made two treaties with the Viking Great Army (868 and 872) only to be driven from it from Repton to exile in Rome, where he died. He was buried in the Church of St Mary in the English quarter.

C

Cadwalla (*c*.658-689) King of Wessex. Reigned from 685 to 688. A member of the Wessex royal family who was forced into exile early in life. He returned in 684 and after establishing himself in Wessex attacked and subjugated the kingdom of Sussex. He also annexed the Isle of Wight and made advances as far as Kent. He was converted to Christianity and after he abdicated made a pilgrimage to Rome where he was baptised in the presence of the pope.

Cadwallon (d.633) King of Gwynedd. Reigned from *c*.625 to 633. An ally of King PENDA of Mercia, he helped defeat King EDWIN of Northumbria in a battle at Hatfield Chase, near Doncaster in 633. He was killed at Hexham by Edwin's nephew, OSWALD, who had returned from exile among the Scots.

Canute (*c*.994-1035) King of England, Denmark and Norway. Reigned (England) from 1014 to 1035. The son of SWEYN FORKBEARD. Following the death of ETHELRED, the kingdom of England fell into confusion and Canute renewed Danish attacks. He began by devastating the eastern coast, and extended his ravages in the south, where, however, he failed to establish himself until after the battle of Ashingdon and the assassination of the Saxon choice for king, EDMUND IRONSIDE. He was accepted as king of the whole of England in 1016. At Harold's death in 1018 he gained Denmark and in 1031 he conquered Norway, thus becoming ruler of a great Danish empire. MALCOLM III of Scotland also admitted Canute's superiority and Sweden also was vassal to him.

Canute, who began his reign with barbarity and crime, afterwards became a humane and wise monarch. He restored the English customs at a general assembly, and ensured to the Danes and English equal rights and equal protection of person and property, and even preferred English subjects to the most important posts. His power was confirmed by his marriage with Emma of Normandy, Ethelred's widow. He died at Shaftesbury, leaving Norway to his eldest son, Sweyn, England to HAROLD and Denmark to the third, HARDICANUTE.

Significant events of Canute's reign

- 1016 – Edmund Ironside is chosen as king by the Saxons.

  Edmund Ironside killed after The Battle of Ashingdon.

  Canute becomes king of all England.

- 1017 – The marriage of Canute and Emma of Normandy.

  Canute creates four earldoms; Wessex, Mercia, Northumbria and East Anglia.

- 1027 – Canute makes a pilgrimage to Rome.

Caradoc (d.*c*.54) King of the Catuvellauni tribe. A
son of Cunobelinus, he resisted the Romans (by whom
he was known as **Caratacus**) from AD 43 to 47 but
was eventually captured and taken to Rome in
chains. His brother Togodummus was probably killed
at the Battle of the Medway in AD 43.

Cartimandua (*fl*.70) Queen of the Brigantes tribe. A
leader of one of the largest British tribes which had
York as its centre.

Caswallon (d.c.60) High king of the British tribes.
Leader of the Catuvellauni tribe which settled in
what is now Hertfordshire. He fought rival tribes to
become high king and united them against the first
Roman invasions.

Cathal O'Connor (d.1224) King of Connaught.
Reigned from 120 to 1224. The last provincial monarch in Ireland. He resisted the advances of Henry III
until his death.

Ceawlin (d.*c*.593) King of Wessex. Reigned from 577
to 591. The son of Cynric, he succeeded his father to
the leadership of the West Saxons and began advancing north of the Thames. In 577 he defeated
Ethelbert of Kent at Wibbandum, killing two of his
sons, and was recognized as *Bretwalda*, overlord of
all the Anglo-Saxon kings. His turbulent reign came
to an end following a power struggle in Wessex and
he died in exile.

Cenfus King of Wessex. Reigned in 674. A grandson
of Ceolwulf.

Cenred King of Mercia. Reigned from 716 to 718. He succeeded the murdered King OSRED.

Centwine King of Wessex. He reigned from 676 to 685. A brother of CENWAHL.

Cenwahl King of Wessex. Reigned from 643 to 672. The son of CYNEGLIS, Cenwahl married a sister of PENDA but had to flee the Mercian king after abandoning her. He extended his territory after Penda's death and won an important victory in 658 at Peonnan, near Exeter. Advancing further into Devon he is said to have 'put the Britons to flight as far as the sea'. He then lost Oxfordshire to Mercia, which also seized the Isle of Wight and lands in Hampshire, and accepted baptism while in exile at the court of King ANNA of East Anglia. He ended his turbulent reign by going on pilgrimage in Rome; his successor INE followed him thirty-seven years later. In Wessex he built the Old Minster, Winchester (648) and was buried there.

Ceorl King of Mercia. Reigned from c.606 to 626. Related to PYBBA, his daughter married the dominant king of Northumbria, EDWIN.

Ceol King of Wessex. Reigned from 591 to 597. Came to the throne after the abdication of CEAWLIN.

Ceolred King of Mercia. Reigned from 709 to 716. The son of ETHELRED, he succeeded COENRED and earned a reputation as a spoiler of monasteries. He also fought King INE of Wessex at Woodborough in Wiltshire in 715.

Ceolwulf (d.760) King of Northumbria. Reigned from 729 to 737. A brother of CENRED, he was temporarily deposed in 731 when a rival faction seized him and had him tonsured as a monk. Bede's *Ecclesiastical History of the English People* was dedicated to him.

Ceolwulf King of Wessex. Reigned from 597 to 611. He succeeded his brother, CEOL, and in 607 defeated the South Saxons who had gained lands in the kingdom following the abdication of CEAWLIN.

Ceolwulf I King of Mercia. Reigned from 821 to 823. Succeeded his brother, COENWULF, but reigned for only two years before being deposed by BEORNWULF.

Ceolwulf II King of Mercia. Reigned from 874 to c.880. The last Mercian king was chosen by the Danish overlords to rule the subordinate western half of the kingdom. He was deposed.

Cerdic King of Wessex. Reigned from 519 to 534. Recorded as the first king of the West Saxons, he landed near Southampton in 494 and fought the Britons for control of the area. He is known to have killed a British king in 508 and had a further victory at Charford on the Avon in 519. By 530 he also had control of the Isle of Wight. His son, CYNRIC, succeeded him.

Charles I (1600-1649) King of Great Britain and Ireland. Reigned from 1625 to 1649. The son of JAMES I (JAMES VI of Scotland) and Anne, daughter of King Ferdinand II of Denmark. Charles was born at Dunfermline Palace (the last sovereign to be born in

Scotland), and was never expected to become king as he was second in line to the throne after his brother, Henry, Prince of Wales. He became heir apparent after his brother died and was created Prince of Wales at the age of twelve. In early 1625, he succeeded to the throne and was crowned at Westminster Abbey. In the same year he was married by proxy to Henrietta Maria, daughter of Henry IV of France.

Charles proved himself to have inherited his father's inflexible convictions about the role of the monarchy in relation to Parliament. As he had Catholic sympathies he favoured the new High Church party of William Laud, soon to be made Archbisop of Canterbury, against the dominant parliamentarians of the time. The first Parliament which he summoned, being more disposed to state grievances than grant supplies, was dissolved after financially crippling Charles. The next year (1626) a new Parliament was summoned; but the House proved no more tractable than before, and it too was soon dissolved. In 1628 a series of military and naval disasters compelled the king to call a new Parliament, which showed itself as much opposed to arbitrary measures as its predecessor, and after voting the supplies prepared the Petition of Rights. This was essentially a reminder to Charles of what the Parliament took to be the traditional liberties of the people and asserted that any loan or tax forced by the king was illegal without the permission of Parliament. Charles was constrained to pass the Petition into law. But the assassination of the Duke of Buckingham, Charles's supporter, and the determined spirit with which the Parliament resisted the king's claim to levy tonnage and poundage on his own authority led to a rupture, and Charles again dissolved the Parliament, resolving to try and reign without one. In this endeavour he was supported by Strafford and Laud as his chief counsellors. With their help Charles continued eleven years without summoning a Parliament, using the arbitrary courts of High Commission and Star Chamber as a kind of cover for pure absolutism, and raising money by unconstitutional or doubtful means. He made various attempts to get estates into his possession on the pretext of invalid titles, and in May 1635, the city of London estates were sequestered. In 1637 John Hampden began the career of resistance to the king's arbitrary measures by refusing to pay ship-money, the right to levy which, without authority of Parliament, he was determined to bring before a court of law. His cause was argued for twelve days in the Court of Exchequer; and although he lost it by the decision of eight of the judges out of twelve, the discussion of the question produced a very powerful impression on the public mind.

During this period Laud began to enforce his High Church discipline and Puritans, forced into exile, founded colonies in America. It was in Scotland, however, that Charles's insensitivity and arrogance came to the fore. Charles was crowned in Edinburgh with full Anglican ceremonial in 1633, and this lost him the goodwill of a number of his Scottish subjects. In 1636 the new Book of Canons was issued by the king's authority, and this attempt of Charles to introduce an Anglican liturgy into Scotland produced great opposition. The Presbyterian nobility in Scotland attempted to obstruct this imposition in Parliament but soon found that the influence of the bishops was too great. The following year saw the introduction of the Book of Common Prayer and it became apparent that Charles was acting without consultation. After repeated petitions to the king frustration led to the drawing up and subscription of the National Covenant in 1638. Thousands gathered in Edinburgh to sign this declaration of faith and obedience to the reformed religion of Scotland. Soon the Covenanters were buying arms and preparing to defend their beliefs on the battlefield and Charles was forced to seek a settlement. Suspension of the Code and Prayer Book and the calling of a General Assembly in Glasgow did not calm the Covenanters however, and they proceeded to abolish episcopacy and defy Charles by refusing to disarm. Charles attempted to reassert himself by force of arms but lack of money and troops frustrated his efforts. He was also forestalled by the effective deployment of men and arms by the Covenant army and hostilities did not immediately begin. Charles sought instead, through an agreement reached at Berwick, to begin consultations with a view to negotiating a peaceful settlement.

The Covenanters would not disband however, and were adamant over the abolition of the bishops. In 1640 a Parliament was summoned and Charles tried again to get military support. Again he was disappointed and an army of Covenanters moved south, taking Newcastle and occupying the northern English counties, remaining there until Charles paid an indemnity to secure their return north. Again Parliament was summoned and the stormy sessions which followed resulted in Charles agreeing to the Act of Attainder under which Charles's chief minister, the Earl of Stafford, was executed. In early 1642 Charles decided to resist and attempted to arrest the Parliamentary leaders. He failed, the City of London gave refuge to the Parliamentarians and Charles left his capital to raise the Royal standard in Nottingham in August. The king had on his side the great bulk of the gentry, while nearly all the Puritans and the inhabitants of the great trading towns sided with the Parliament.

The early successes of the king resulted in Parliament making a Solemn League and Covenant with the Scots, in return for whose help they promised to impose Presbyterianism on England. The first action, the battle of Edgehill, gave the king a slight advantage; but nothing very decisive happened until the battle of Marston Moor, in 1644. The Parliamentary army by this stage was composed of Scots, Roundheads and Sir Thomas Fairfax and Oliver Cromwell's New Model Army. The latter army fought with great vigour, representing as it did the fervour of the extreme Puritan sects, and went on to route the Royalists at the battle of Naseby. This completed the ruin of the king's cause and Charles at length gave himself up to the Scottish army at Newark. The Parliamentarians who favoured moderation in the face of mounting religious extremism had been displaced by Cromwell however, and when the Scots decided to surrender Charles they had little influence on his fate. When the moderate Covenanters realized that their hopes for a Presbyterian settlement in England would be better served by a having a legitimate sovereign than by the turbulent Cromwell, they rallied in support of Charles. The 'Engagement' was a failure however, and the defeat of the Royalist army at Preston (1648) sealed the King's fate. Cromwell was soon able to coerce Parliament and the more hesitating of the Presbyterians into bringing Charles to trial for high treason against the people.

Although Charles repeatedly refused to recognise the court he had the sentence of death pronounced against him. All interposition being in vain, he was beheaded before the Banqueting House in Whitehall, meeting his fate with an admirable obstinacy that seemed dignified and courageous. The execution of the king produced a feeling of revulsion throughout the country and Cromwell had to maintain his minority rule by force.

Charles had nine children, notably CHARLES II and JAMES VII. He was buried at St George's Chapel, Windsor Castle.

Significant events of Charles I's reign

- 1626 – Parliament dismissed by Charles.
- 1627 – England declares war on France.
- 1628 – Assassination of Buckingham.

- 1628 – Charles reluctantly agreed the Petition
  of Rights.

- 1629 – Charles dismisses Parliament again, this
  time for eleven years.

- 1632 – Van Dyck becomes Court painter.

- 1637 – A new Book of Common Prayer in
  published.

- 1638 – National Covenant pledged in Scotland.

- 1640 – The Short Parliament (3 weeks) is called.
  The Long Parliament (until 1660) is
  called.

- 1641 – Abolition of the Star Chamber.

- 1642 – Civil War begins.

- 1644 – Solemn League and Covenant signed.
  Battle of Marston Moor.

- 1645 – Battle of Naseby.

- 1646 – Scots surrender Charles to English
  Parliament.

- 1648 – Royalist Scots invade England.

- 1649 – England is declared a republic.
  Parliament tries and executes Charles.

Charles II (1630-1685) King of Great Britain and Ireland. Reigned from 1660 to 1685. The eldest surviving son of CHARLES I and Henrietta Maria of France and the brother of James, Duke of York, later JAMES VII. He was sent into exile in France after the battle of Edgehill (1645) and was there tutored by Thomas Hobbes among others. After his father's execution he immediately assumed the royal title. At the time, however, Cromwell was all-powerful in England and he accepted an invitation from the Scots, who had proclaimed him their king. He sailed from Holland and was crowned at Scone (1651) making him the last king to be crowned in Scotland. It would still be ten years before the restoration of the monarchy in England, but in Scotland at least the Stuart succession remained unbroken, although Charles never revisited Scotland after1660.

An early attempt to take back the throne was frustrated by divisions among the Royalist parties and Charles reluctantly had to sign the Covenant to appease the strongest faction. Eventually he took to the field with the English Royalists, who, having gathered an army, encountered Cromwell at Worcester and were totally defeated. With great difficulty Charles escaped to France. Richard Cromwell succeeded his father in 1658 but almost immediately abdicated in the face of growing discontent with the Puritan austerities of the time. The popular Restoration, effected without a struggle by General Monk, set Charles on the throne after the Declaration of Breda, his entry into the capital being made amidst universal acclamations.

He was a witty and stylish man, and seemed at first to characterize the anti-Puritan mood of the country, becoming known by many as the 'Merry Monarch'. Within two years he married the Infanta of Portugal, Catherine of Braganza, and for a time his measures, mainly counselled by the Chancellor Lord Clarendon, were prudent and conciliatory. In this favourable climate Charles re-established much of the royal pre-rogative. The privileges of the Anglican Church were restored and a pro-Catholic policy began to appear, excluding Nonconformists from holding municipal office and forcing Puritans to accept the doctrines of the Church of England. But the extravagance and licentious habits of the king soon involved the nation as well as himself in difficulties. Dunkirk was sold to the French to relieve his pecuniary embarrassment, and war, caused by commercial rivalry, broke out with Holland. A Dutch fleet entered the Thames, and burned and destroyed ships as far up as Chatham. The great plague in 1663, and the great fire of London which burned 13,000 houses to the ground the year following, added to the disasters of the period. Amid such calamities there were mutterings of idolatry having taken root in the in a licentious court.

A triple alliance between England, Holland and Sweden, for the purpose of checking the ambition of Louis XIV, followed, but the extravagance of the king made him willing to become a mere pensioner of Louis XIV with whom he arranged a private treaty in 1670. This was the Secret Treaty of Dover by which he declared himself a Catholic and agreed to restore Catholicism in return for secret subsidies from Louis XIV of France. After this Charles issued a declaration attempting to free both Protestant dissenters and Roman Catholics from some of their disabilities. Parliament countered this with the Test Act which was designed to keep Roman Catholics out of Public office. In 1674 Parliament also reversed

Charles's foreign policy by breaking off relations with France and making peace with the Dutch.

Alarm over the 'Popish Plot' of 1678, in which an Anglican parson, Titus Oates, disclosed a Catholic plot to murder Charles and restore Catholicism to England led to further difficulties between Charles and Parliament. The plot was soon revealed to be a fabrication but the resulting furore led Parliament to attempt to exclude Charles's Catholic brother from the throne. The question of the succession was only settled after the passing of the Habeas Corpus Act in 1679 which established important measures for protecting individual rights. A new Parliament which assembled in 1680 had to be dissolved following further difficulties with the king, and yet another which met the following year at Oxford. Finally Charles, like his father, determined to govern without a Parliament, and after the discovery of an assassination conspiracy (the Rye House plot of 1683) and the execution of Lord Russell and Algernon Sidney, Charles became as absolute as any sovereign in Europe although political stability was maintained until his death in 1685. England, however, was deeply divided and uncertain of the future and thus unable to take a full part in European affairs. Advances were nonetheless made during his reign in the fields of science and architecture, areas in which Charles took great interest, encouraging and supporting the work of men like Newton, Boyle and Wren.

Charles II died from the consequences of an apoplectic fit in early 1685 after converting to Catholicism on his deathbed and having received the sacrament according to the rites of the Roman Church. He had no legitimate children but was well-known for his love of women; his many mistresses included the famous Nell Gwynn and several others were raised to the highest ranks of nobility. Six of the thirteen illegitimate sons he had by them were made dukes; Monmouth (by Lucy Walters), St Albans (by Nell Gwynn), Richmond (by Louise de Querouaille), and Cleveland, Grafton and Northumberland (by Barbara Villiers).

Significant events of Charles II's reign

- 1660 – The Restoration of Charles to the throne.

     Samuel Pepys diary is begun.

- 1661 – Parliament meets at Westminster.

- 1662 – Act of Uniformity compels Puritans to accept the Church of England doctrines.

     The Royal Society receives its charter.

- 1665 – Two year long war begins with Holland.

     London struck by plague.

- 1666 – The Great Fire of London.

- 1670 – The Secret Treaty of Dover with France.

- 1672 – War resumes with Holland.

- 1673 – Test Act introduced to keep Catholics from office.

- 1675 – Creation of the Royal Observatory.

     The building of St Paul's Cathedral is begun.

- 1678 – The Popish Plot results in the persecution of the Catholics.
- 1679 – The Habeus Corpus Act introduced.

  Whig and Tory first used as names for political parties.
- 1681 – Exclusion Bill attempts to exclude James from the succession.
- 1683 – Rye House Plot to murder the king is uncovered.
- 1685 – Charles converts to Catholicism on his deathbed.

Cinioch (d.631) King of Picts. Son of GARTNART's sister, the dates of his reign are not known.

Ciniod King of Picts. He reigned from 763 to 775. Son of OENGUS's sister.

Cissa King of Sussex. Reigned from c.514. Participated in the siege of Pevensey in 491 and succeeded his father AELLE. He gave his name to Chichester (Cissa's-ceaster), the royal capital. Nothing more is known of him as the *Anglo-Saxon Chronicle* does not mention the South Saxons again until 661.

Coel (Old Coel the Splendid) (*fl.*420) British tribal king. The 'Old King Cole' of nursery rhyme fame was overlord of several British tribes and ruled much of lowland Scotland. His descendants ruled the kingdom of Strathclyde.

Coenred King of Mercia. Reigned from 704 to 709. The eldest son of WULFHERE. On his father's death the throne was taken by ETHELRED as he was then too young to rule. In 697 there were rebellions south of the Humber and he was declared king there in 702. Two years later Ethelred died and Coenred succeeded him as king of Mercia. He was unsuited to the royal life, however, and abdicated in 709 in favour of Ethelred's son, CEOLRED. Soon after he left England to become a monk in Rome and dedicated the rest of his life to spiritual works.

Coenwulf King of Mercia. Reigned from 796 to 821. A descendant of PENDA's youngest brother. Worcestershire is first mentioned in a land grant he made to Bishop Deneberht sometime between 814 and 820.

Cogidummus (*fl.*75) King of the Regni tribe. A client king of the Romans, he called himself the legate of the Emperor in Britain and built himself a palace at Fishbourne, near Chichester.

Commius (*fl.*50) King of the Atrebates tribe. Leader of the tribe which settled in what are now Hampshire and Sussex after fleeing Gaul.

Conall King of Picts. Reigned from 787 to 789. The son of ALPIN II's sister, he succeeded TALORGEN but was deposed within two years by CONSTANTINE.

Constantine (d.820) King of Picts. Reigned from 789 to 820. The first Constantine to rule in Scotland was the son of ALPIN II's sister. He asserted his authority over the Scots of Dalriada sometime after 811, a task which was made easier by the frequent Viking attacks of the period.

Constantine I (d.878) King of Scots. Reigned from
862 to 877. Thought to have been the son of KENNETH
MAC-ALPIN, he succeeded Kenneth's brother, DONALD,
to the throne and bore the title of Constantine I although he was not the first king of that name in Scotland. During his reign his kingdom was frequently
attacked by Viking forces sailing from Ireland. Following a landing in Fife in 879 his forces were routed
at Dollar and in a further engagement at Forgan he
lost his life. He was succeeded by his brother, AED,
who soon after was murdered by a rival to the throne.
Constantine's sister had married RUN, the British
king of Strathclyde and their son, EOCHA, became king
after Aed.

Constantine II (d.952) King of Scots. Reigned from
900 to 952. After defeating the Danes, who had killed
his predecessor, DONALD II, he held an Ecclesiastical
Court at Scone for the settlement of the rule and discipline of the Celtic Church. In diplomatic affairs he
was the first Scottish king to acknowledge an English
king as overlord (EDWARD THE ELDER, son of ALFRED
THE GREAT, in 924) but this may only have been for
expediency, as an ally against Norse aggression. An
invasion by ETHELSTAN, son of Edward, led to a counter invasion by the Scots which resulted in the Battle
of Brunanburgh, near the Humber, in 937. The
Northumbrians were the victors despite Constantine
having received the assistance of a Norse force from
Dublin. He abdicated in 942, leaving the throne to his
cousin MALCOLM I, and spent the final years of his
life as an Abbot at St Andrews.

Constantine III (d.997) King of Scots. Reigned from 995 to 997. The grandson of CONSTANTINE II and son of CUILEAN, his reign was short and turbulent. It is thought he may have been murdered by KENNETH III in 997 after having had KENNETH II murdered two years previously.

Cormac mac-Art (d.*c*.360) High king of Ireland. A semi-legendary warrior king who reigned from Tara, where he is said to have quarrelled with the local Druids after converting to Christianity. He choked to death on a fishbone and folklore has it that a Druid curse was to blame.

Creoda (d.593) King of Mercia. He reigned from *c*.585 to 593. The first named king of the Mercians, he is thought to have been the son of Icel, the first continental Angle king to settle in Britain.

Cuilean (d.971) King of Scots. Ruled from 966 to 971. He was killed in battle fighting the Britons of Strathclyde.

Cunedda (*fl*.390) Welsh tribal king. A chieftain settled by the Romans in north Wales where he defended the country against attacks from Ireland. Kings of Gwynedd claim descent from him.

Cunobelinus (*fl*.43) High king of the British tribes. The Shakespearean *Cymbeline*. He was recognized by Augustus as the leader of the Catuvellauni tribe and high king of many others. He became an ally of the Romans and ruled from Camulodunum (Colchester). His sons later resisted the Romans.

Cuthred King of Wessex (d.756). Reigned from 740 to 756. He defeated ETHELBALD of Mercia at Burford in Oxfordshire in 752.

Cyneglis (d.641) King of Wessex. Reigned from 611 to 643. He failed in a plot to murder EDWIN of Northumbria in 626 and in 628 he was defeated in a territorial dispute with PENDA of Mercia. Towards the end of his reign he was converted to Christianity.

Cynewulf (d.786) King of Wessex. Reigned from 757 to 786. A client of OFFA of Mercia, he was murdered while visiting his mistress by CYNEHEARD, a brother of SIGEBERT of Wessex, who believed that he was plotting to exile him. Cyneheard was killed by Cynewul's bodyguards.

Cynric King of Wessex. Reigned from 534 to 560. He extended his kingdom by fighting the Britons at Salisbury in 552 and at Barbury, near Swindon in 556. He was succeeded by his son, CEAWLIN.

D

Dafydd ap Llywelyn (d.1246) King of Gwynedd. Reigned from 1240 to 1246. The second son and successor of LLYWELYN the Great. He attempted to take back lands lost to the English but was forced to do homage to HENRY III and give up all the territories won by his father since 1215. He titled himself 'Prince of Wales' in 1244 and died after uniting other Welsh rulers in a second attempt to restore the kingdom. The Baron's War in England enabled him to marry Simon de Montford's daughter in 1278 but he died without an heir and his principality was divided among the sons of his elder brother.

Dafydd ap Opwain (d.1194) King of Gwynedd. Reigned from 1170 to 1194. He married HENRY II's illegitimate half-sister, Emma.

David I (the Saint) (c1081-1153) King of Scots. Reigned from 1124 to 1153. The sixth son of MALCOLM III Canmore's second marriage to Margaret, sister of Edgar the Aetheling. His early years were spent at the English court of HENRY I and in 1100 his sister married the king; their daughter became Queen Matilda. On the death of his elder brother EDGAR, David inherited that part of Scotland below the Forth-Clyde line. However another brother, ALEXANDER I, succeeded Edgar and he disputed the right of David to this territory until David strengthened his position with the support of Henry. At Alexander's death in 1124 he quickly established himself throughout his kingdom by initiating a simple form of centralized government. He was the first to introduce feudal institutions to his native land and was the first Scottish king to strike his own coinage. He also vigorously promoted education and agriculture and regularly gave informal audience to the poor in all the languages of the realm. During David's reign around a dozen royal burghs were created including Perth and Aberdeen.

Amidst baronial revolts in England David twice took an army south to support his niece Matilda against STEPHEN, her rival claimant for the English crown; during one of his incursions he was defeated at the Battle of the Standard near Northallerton in Yorkshire (1138).

David also acquired a considerable reputation for sanctity. While Prince of Cumbria he had begun the re-establishment or restoration of the Glasgow bishopric, and after he became king founded the bishoprics of Aberdeen, Ross, Caithness, Brechin, and Dunblane. Among the religious houses which date from his reign are Holyrood, Melrose, Jedburgh, Kelso, Dryburgh, and Newbattle. His services to the Church procured for him the popular title of saint, but the endowments so taxed the royal domains and possessions that JAMES VI famously characterized him as 'ane sair sanct for the crown'.

In old age he spent his time gardening and establishing apple orchards. He died at Carlisle in 1153, and was succeeded by his eldest grandson, who, as MALCOLM III, inherited a peaceful and flourishing kingdom.

David II (1324-1371) King of Scots. Reigned with interruptions from 1329 to 1371. David was born at Dunfermline, the son of ROBERT I (the Bruce) by his second wife, Elizabeth de Burgh. At the age of four he was married to Joan, sister of EDWARD III of England, then only three years older. He succeeded to the throne on the death of his father and was acknowledged as king by the greater part of the nation.

During his minority he was troubled by those his father had disinherited and who supported the claim of EDWARD BALLIOL, the son of JOHN BALLIOL, to the throne. Balliol was backed by Edward III of England, and at first was successful at the Battle of Dupplin Moor, being coronated at Scone soon after. David fled to France following a later defeat at Halidon Hill but eventually returned to Scotland at the age of seventeen and succeeded in driving Balliol from Scotland. Still, however, the war was carried on with England with increasing rancour, till at length David was wounded and made prisoner at the Battle of Neville's Cross, near Durham (1346). After being detained in captivity for eleven years, he was ransomed for 100,000 merks, to be paid in annual instalments, but in place of making the payments he made the offer of leaving his kingdom to an English heir. Following opposition from his nobles, this plan was disallowed by the Scottish Parliament who disliked the idea of a formal union of the crowns.

David married Margaret Drummond in 1363 following the death of Joan, but died at Edinburgh Castle seven years later without having produced an heir.

Significant events of David II's reign

- 1332 – David deposed by John Balliol.
- 1333 – Edward III invades Scotland.
- 1341 – David II returns to claim the throne.
- 1346 – Battle of Neville's Cross. David captured and held in the Tower of London.
- 1348 – Scotland afflicted by the Black Death.
- 1357 – The Treaty of Berwick. David returns to Scotland.
- 1363 – David II offers the Scottish throne to Edward III.

Donald I (d.862) King of Scots. Reigned from 858 to 862. The son of ALPIN and brother of KENNETH I. He reputedly applied the laws of Dalriada to Pictland. Donald died at Scone leaving the throne to Kenneth I's son, CONSTANTINE.

Donald II (d.900) King of Scots. Reigned from 889 to 900. The son of CONSTANTINE I, he was the first king of both the Scots and Picts to be referred to as *ri alban* or King of Alba. His kingdom was repeatedly ravaged by the Norse and he was killed in battle near Dunnottar. He was succeeded by CONSTANTINE II.

Donald III Bane (1031-1100) King of Scots. Reigned from 1093 to 1100. Donald, whose sobriquet 'Bane' means 'fair', retreated to the Hebrides on the death of his father DUNCAN I at the hands of his rival, MACBETH; Donald's brother, later MALCOLM III, took refuge in England. Macbeth was himself overthrown (1054) and killed by Malcolm who then became King of Scots. During his exile in the Hebrides Donald Bane had been exposed to Celtic culture and, under Malcolm's rule, had nursed a hatred of the increasing English influence he saw in the Scottish court. On Malcolm's death Donald seized the throne, at the age of 62, and attempted to reverse the anglicisation of the court. His position was soon threatened, however, by Malcolm's son, DUNCAN, who had been trained as a Norman knight during his period of detention as a hostage in England. An invasion led by Duncan, with the backing of an English and French army, dethroned Donald in 1094 but Donald regained the throne when Edmund, another of Malcolm's sons, killed Duncan. Malcolm's other surviving son, EDGAR, then had Donald blinded and imprisoned in 1097. He died three years later and became the last Scottish king to be buried on Iona.

Donald Breac (d.642) King of Scots. Reigned c635 to 642. The tenth king of Dalriada, he invaded Ireland in 636 and was soundly beaten at the battle of Magh Rath (Moira). This was said to have activated the curse of St Columba on Scots kings who fought their own kinsmen. After returning to Scotland he was killed in a battle with the Strathclyde Britons at

Strathcarron in 642. These defeats led to a sharp decline in the influence of Dalriada in Scotland.

Drest I King of Picts. Reigned from 663 to 671. The brother of GARTNAIT, he was ousted by a faction of the Picts who resented the influence and expansionist policies of his uncle, EGFRITH, the Northumbrian king. He was succeeded by BRIDEI III who crushed Egfrith's army at Nechtansmere in 685.

Drest II (d.729) King of Picts. Reigned from 724 to 729. The son of NECHTON's sister, he was one of four who claimed the title of king in 724 following the decision of Nechtan to abdicate. He was killed by his cousin OENGUS in 729.

Drest III (d.780) King of Picts. Reigned in 780. The son of ALPIN II's sister.

Drest IV (d.837) King of Picts. Reigned from 834 to 837. He was the son of UEN.

Drust (d.848) King of Picts. Reigned from 845 to 848. One of the sons of UURAD.

Duff (d.966) King of Scots. Reigned from 962 to 966. The son of MALCOLM I, he was killed in battle.

Duncan I (1010-1040) King of Scots. Reigned from 1034 to 1040. The son of Crinan, Abbot of Dunkeld, and Bethoc, daughter of MALCOLM II, Duncan succeeded his grandfather and founded the Dunkeld dynasty. When he became king of Scots he was already the king of Strathclyde and therefore inherited a kingdom larger than any held by his predecessors. A rash and hot-headed king, he was not particularly successful in battle and in 1039 fruitlessly besieged Durham. He was also twice defeated in battle by his cousin Thorfinn, Earl of Orkney, before being killed by a rival for the throne, MACBETH, mormaer, or steward, of Moray at Forres, near Elgin, in 1040. He married a cousin of the Earl of Northumberland and had two sons who both became kings; MALCOLM III CANMORE and DONALD BANE. After their father's murder the two brothers fled the kingdom.

Duncan II (1060-1094) King of Scots. Reigned in 1094. The eldest son of MALCOLM III from his first marriage. His father had given him as a hostage to WILLIAM II in 1072 and he grew up in Normandy before being set free and knighted in 1087. Soon after he married Octreda of Northumberland. On the death of his father he was seen as the true heir and with support from the English king, William II, under whose banners he was then serving, led an Anglo-Norman army north. He defeated his uncle DONALD BANE to become king but his reign was short and difficult as there was much resentment of his English supporters. Within a matter of months he was slain in battle by his half-brother, Edmund, at Mondynes near Dunnotter and Donald Bane regained power. Donald was soon after deposed by another of Malcolm's sons, EDGAR.

Dyfnwal (d.934) King of Strathclyde. Reigned c920 to 934. He recognized the Wessex king, EDWARD the Elder, as overlord in 925.

Dyfnwal (d.975) King of Strathclyde. Reigned from 934 to *c*.973. He killed the king of Scots, CUILEAN, in battle in 971 and died whilst on a pilgrimage to Rome.

E

Eadbert (d.768) King of Northumbria. Reigned from 737 to 758. Came to the throne after the abdication of his cousin CEOLWULF. His brother, Egbert, had been made Archbishop of York and they governed Church and state in union. In 740 he led a campaign against the Picts and in his absence ETHELBERT, King of Mercia, ravaged parts of his kingdom. He soon recovered his lands and went on to add parts of Strathclyde to his kingdom. In 756 he was defeated by the Strathclyde Britons and two years later he resigned his crown in favour of his son, OSWULF. Soon after he entered the monastry of St Peters at York and remained there until his death.

Eadbert I (d.748) King of Kent. Reigned from 725 to 748. Joint ruler of the kingdom with his brother, ETHELBERT II.

Eadbert II Praen (d.c810) King of Kent. Reigned from 796 to 798. Despite having had received the tonsure, Eadbert strongly contested the Mercian domination of Kent and on the death of OFFA he became king. He was supported by his nobles and condemned by the Church which favoured Mercia. In

798 COENWULF invaded Kent, captured the king, and caused him to have his hands cut off and his eyes burned out. Coenwulf then imposed CUTHRED as an under-king and the independent existence of Kent was brought to an end.

Eadric (d.688) King of Kent. Reigned from *c*.685 to 687. Joint ruler with the East Saxon, SUABHARD, under the overlordship of the South Saxons.

Eanfrith King of Bernicia. Reigned from 633 to 634. The son of Ethelfrith, he married a Pictish princess and their son, TALORCEN, became a king of the Picts. He was killed by the Welsh king, CADWALLON.

Eanred (d.850) King of Northumbria. Reigned from 809 to 841. A son of EARDWULF, he did homage to EGBERT of Wessex in 827.

Eardwulf (d.762) King of Kent. Reigned from 747 to 762. The son of EARDBERT, he was a joint ruler of the kingdom with ETHELBERT II.

Eardwulf King of Northumbria. Reigned from 796 to 809. He deposed OSBALD and was succeeded by his son, ENRED.

Edbald (d.640) King of Kent. Reigned 616 to 640. On succeeding his father, ETHELBERT, he promptly renounced Christianity, which had been introduced to the kingdom by St Augustine in his father's reign. He married his stepmother before taking Emma, daughter of the Frankish King Theudebert II of Austrasia, as his queen.

Edgar (943-975) King of England. Reigned from 957
to 975. The second son of Edmund I and Elgifu, he
replaced Edwy as ruler of Northumbria and Mercia
after nobles who were discontented with his brother
transferred their allegiance. Edwy still held the lands
south of the Thames but this came into Edgar's kingdom following his early death. In 973 he was created
'Emperor of Britain' at a ceremony in Bath conducted by the Archbishop of Canterbury. The same
year he was supposedly rowed on the River Dee by
six or eight kings as an act of subservience. These
kings included Malcolm of Strathclyde, Kenneth II
of Scots, Maccus of the Isle of Man and up to five
Welsh kings. It is probable that this was a conference
to discuss borders in which the Scots recognized
English control over Bernicia in Northumberland in
return for Edgar's acknowledgement of their rule of
the Lothians.

In contrast to his brother he was known for his piety and reinstated Dunstan as Archbishop of Canterbury as well as making him his chief adviser. Acting
under Edgar's patronage Dunstan led a revival of
Benedictine monasticism and reformed the church.
In order to secure the loyalty of his clerics forty abbeys were founded in his reign and laws introduced
which punished non-payment of taxes due to the
Church. He also reformed the administration of the
country, codified the laws of the land and clarified
the boundaries between shires. He also struck a new
coinage and licensed towns to mint the new silver
pennies. He married twice to daughters of his

ealdormen and kept a mistress. His legitimate sons were EDWARD (the Marytr), Edmund (the Aetheling) and ETHELRED II (the Unready).

Edgar (1074-1107) King of Scots. Reigned from 1097 to 1107. The fourth son of MALCOLM III's second marriage. On his father's death he went to the English court where he was sheltered by WILLIAM II. He returned to Scotland in 1096 and with the help of English troops he defeated his uncle DONALD BANE at Roscobie in Fife in early 1097. He became king in October of the same year and afterwards was practically a dependant of William II and HENRY I of England. Shortly after he took the throne his kingdom was threatened by the King of Norway, Magnus Barelegs, who brought a considerable fleet into western waters and forced Edgar to cede 'all the isles around which a ship could sails' including Kintyre. Pursuing a pro-English policy, he settled the first English knight in Lothian and married his sister Matilda to Henry I in 1100. He died unmarried and the kingdom passed to his brother ALEXANDER I. The 'king with the Saxon name' was buried in Dunfermline.

Edmund (St Edmund) (c.840-870) King of East Anglia. Reigned from c.855 to 870. East Anglia's last Anglo-Saxon king was defeated and martyred by Danish invaders at Haegelisdum (Hellesdon in Norwich or Hoxne in Suffolk) in 870. Seeking to avert war he had tried to negotiate with the Danes but his stipulation that they convert to Christianity before making peace offended them. As a consequence on his capture he was subjected to the 'blood eagle' rite and beheaded. He became protector of sailors and for a time was England's patron saint.

Edmund I (921-946) King of England. Reigned from 939 to 946. The eldest son of EDGAR the Elder and Edgifu, he succeeded his half-brother ETHELSTAN as king. Having commanded well at Brunanburgh, Edmund reclaimed those parts of the kingdom lost after his brother's death to Norse King OLAF II. He also subdued Strathclyde which he bestowed on MALCOLM I, King of Scots, on the condition of him doing homage for it. This secured the Anglo-Scottish border. He was slain by Leofa, an exiled thief, while keeping the feast of St Augustine (26th May) of Canterbury at Pucklechurch in 946 and was buried at Glastonbury. His married twice and had two sons who became kings; EDGAR and EDWY.

Edmund II Ironside (993-1016) King of England. Reigned for seven months in 1016. The eldest surviving son of ETHELRED II and Elfled. The warrior prince gained the name 'Ironside' for his bravery against the Danes. He attempted to oppose CANUTE's invasion of Wessex in late 1015 but could not hold Northumbria when Canute moved against it early the following year. On his father's death Edmund was chosen king by a council of Anglo-Saxon kings and ealdormen (the *Witan*) in London and proclaimed in early 1016. Canute, however, had already been elected king by a majority of Witan members gathered at Southamp-

ton. Edmund marched into Wessex and won three of
the four battles there, relieving a besieged London,
but support from the Mercian king EDRIC did not ar-
rive and his cause was lost. He was finally defeated
at Assandun in Essex (1016) and forced to surrender
the midland and northern counties to Canute after a
meeting at Olney where the two rivals agreed to par-
tition England. He died at London of natural causes
(although later sources claim he was murdered) after
a reign of only seven months and was buried at Glastonbury. His infant sons fled Canute's invasion and
settled in Hungary.

Edred (923-955) King of England. Reigned from 946
to 955. The youngest son of EDWARD the Elder and
Edgifu, succeeded to the throne on the murder of his
brother, EDMUND I, in 946 as Edmund's two sons
were too young too reign. Because of ill-health the
government of the kingdom appears to have been
carried out by his mother and his chief minister, the
Abbot Dunstan. Despite his health, Edred was able to
quell a rebellion of the Northumbrian Danes under
ERIK Bloodaxe (948) but it was not until 954 that
Edred was able to secure Northumbria again as part
of his kingdom. This he achieved through a bloody
invasion which resulted in the death of the usurper
king. Edred committed Northumbria to Oswulf as an
earldom. He died while still in his early twenties and
was buried at Winchester.

Edward the Confessor (St Edward) (1003-1066) King
of England. Reigned from 1042 to 1066. The eldest

son of ETHELRED II and Emma of Normandy, he was born at Islip, in Oxfordshire and lived in exile in Normandy from 1013 to 1042 while the Danes ruled England. On the death of his maternal brother, HARDICANUTE the Dane, he was called to the throne and thus renewed the Saxon line.

He restored the Norman influence in England as, not unnaturally, he had returned more French than English, and brought with him his Norman clergy and supporters. He moved the royal residence from the walled city of London to the Palace of Westminster, and this, more than anything else, ensured the return of a Dane to the throne after his death. London had been the wealthiest city in the land and became the centre for discontent with his rule among the powerful anti-Norman party. The real power devolved to his father-in-law, Godwin, the Earl of Wessex, and Edward was forced to remove him from government and place his own Norman supporters in high office. After a dispute in Dover, Godwin left for France in 1051 and returned a year later to take London by force. After a period of confrontation Godwin was reconciled with the king, but died shortly after, leaving his son, HAROLD, to became the Earl of Wessex. Harold returned from exile in Ireland and had little difficulty in assuming his father's position of influence. During Godwin's time in exile however, Edward had appealed for Norman help to reassert his authority and had promised the throne of England to William, Duke of Normandy, in return. There was little support for such a succession in England and on

Edward's death in 1066 Harold took the throne, claiming that his succession had been accepted by the dying king some time beforehand. This was contested by WILLIAM, the Duke of Normandy, who asserted that Edward had confirmed his earlier promise some two years before his death. The succession dispute led directly to the Norman conquest of England.

Edward was a weak and superstitious, but well-intentioned king, who, despite his Norman up-bringing, acquired the respect of his subjects by his monkish sanctity and care in the administration of justice. His legacy was the Abbey at Westminster and he was canonized by Pope Alexander III in 1161.

Edward the Elder (870-924) King of Wessex. Reigned from 899 to 924. The son of ALFRED the Great, he inherited Wessex from his father and defeated a Danish-backed claimant for the throne. His reign was distinguished by a series of successes over the Danes as he took control of the Danish-held Five Boroughs (Nottingham, Derby, Lincoln, Leicester and Stamford). He fortified many inland towns (including Manchester in 919) and acquired dominion over Mercia, which had been allied to his father's kingdom. With Mercian support he extended his authority to run from the English Channel to the Humber. In the north he subdued the Strathclyde king, DYFNWAL, and several Welsh tribes who later sought his protection from the Norse. Among his many sons and daughters by three wives were ELFWARD, ETHELSTAN, EDMUND and EDRED, who all became kings. He was buried at Winchester New Minster.

Edward the Martyr (St Edward) (963-978) King of England. Reigned from 975 to 978. The only son of EDGAR and his first wife, Ethelfled, he succeeded his father at the age of twelve. His succession was disputed by supporters of Edgar's second son by his second wife, ETHELRED, and he began his reign amid a power struggle. The opportunity was taken by some members of the royal court to regain the power lost when Edgar increased the land-holding and authority of the Church. Attacks on monasteries and Church property by secular landowners became more frequent, especially in the north of the country where it was compounded by opposition to southern rule. Edward was guided by the powerful Archbishop Dunstan but seemed powerless to stop the seizures of monastic estates and other church lands.

He was treacherously slain after only three years on the throne by a servant of his stepmother at her residence, Corfe Castle in Dorset. Travelling alone to the castle, he was seized from behind while waiting at the gates and stabbed. It is generally held that his stepmother ordered the assassination in order to make Ethelred king. The pity caused by his innocence and misfortune induced the people to regard him as a martyr and miracles supposed to occur at his tomb later led him to be venerated as a saint

Edward I (Hammer of the Scots) (1239-1307) King of England, Wales, Scotland and Ireland. Reigned from 1272 to 1307. The eldest surviving son of HENRY III and Eleanor of Provence. The contests between his father and the barons called him early into active life.

By 1265 Simon de Montford had become leader of
the opposition to King Henry and formed a Parliament which represented, not only the knights of the
shires, but the burgesses of the towns which supported him as well. Prince Edward restored the royal
authority within months by defeating and killing de
Montford at the Battle of Eavesham. He then proceeded to Palestine, where he showed signal proofs
of valour, although no conquest of any importance
was achieved. He returned on his father's death after
further campaigns in Italy and France with a reputation as an excellent soldier and was crowned amid
much public rejoicing at Westminster Abbey in 1274.
The new king was immediately popular among the
people as he identified himself with the growing tide
of nationalism which was sweeping the country. The
other side to this popular nationalism was displayed
later in his persecution and banishment of the Jews
which was the culmination of many years of anti-
semitism in England. The spirit of nationalism also
led to England looking to its borders. The mountain-
ous land to the west had never been completely subdued, and following an uprising against English influence Edward commenced a war with LLEWELLYN,
Prince of Wales, which ended in the annexation of
that Principality to the English Crown in 1283. He
secured the new Principality of England by building
nine castles along the border and created his eldest
son, Edward, Prince of Wales in 1301.

From the earliest days of his reign Edward showed
great vigour as well as a degree of severity in his ad-

ministration, especially in his policy of limiting the encroachment of the barons and the Church. This was achieved by restricting baronial privileges and prohibiting gifts of land to the Church. His harsh treatment of those in power that he found to be corrupt also gave him the support of the common people and his reforms of the administration were brought about only with their backing. Under his guidance the great common law courts consisting of the King's Bench, Exchequer and Common pleas took shape. He also called the Model Parliament which, with nobles, Churchmen and commoners, foreshadowed representative government.

Edward's great ambition however, was to gain possession of Scotland, but the death of MARGARET, the Maid of Norway, who was to have been married to Edward's son, for a time frustrated the king's designs. The contested succession soon gave him the opportunity to intervene however, and he was invited by the Scots to choose between the thirteen competitors for the throne. His choice, JOHN BALLIOL, was induced to do homage for his crown to Edward at Newcastle but was forced by the indignation of the Scottish people to throw off Edward's overlordship. An alliance between the French and the Scots followed and Edward, then at war with the French king over possession of Gascony, marched his army north. He entered Scotland in 1296, devastated it with fire and sword, which earned him the sobriquet 'Hammer of the Scots' and removed the symbolic 'Stone of Destiny' from Scone.

Edward assumed the administration of the country but the following summer a new rising took place under William Wallace, the son of a knight. His successes, notably at Stirling Bridge, recalled Edward to Scotland with an army of 100,000 men. After defeating Wallace's army at Falkirk the supporters of Scottish independence went into hiding but their leader was at length betrayed and executed in London as a traitor. The unjust and barbaric execution of Wallace made him a national hero in his homeland and resistance to England became paramount among the people. All Edward's efforts to reduce the country to obedience were unavailing and with the crowning of Robert Bruce, Earl of Carrick, as ROBERT I of Scotland, the banner of independence was again unfurled. In 1306 an enraged Edward assembled another army and marched against Bruce, but only reached Burgh-on-sands, a village near Carlisle, where he died.

He was married twice; to Eleanor of Castile, by whom he had sixteen children, and Margaret of France by whom he had three. Twelve memorials to his first wife stand between Nottingham and London to mark the journey taken by the funeral cortege. He was buried at Westminster Abbey.

Significant events of Edward I's reign

- 1277 – Edward mounts an invasion of Wales.

- 1282 – Llywelyn, the last independent Prince of Wales, is killed at Builth.

- 1284 – The Statute of Rhuddlan brings Wales under English rule.

- 1285 – The first Justices of the Peace installed.
- 1290 – England banishes the Jews.

  Margaret, Maid of Norway, dies before reaching Scotland.
- 1292 – John Balliol is chosen by Edward to become Scotland's king.
- 1295 – The Model Parliament is assembled. Edward mounts an invasion of France.
- 1296 – The Scots are vanquished by Edward's invading army and Balliol is deposed.
- 1297 – William Wallace gains victory over Edward at Stirling Bridge.
- 1298 – Wallace defeated at Battle of Falkirk.
- 1301 – Edward makes his son, Edward, the Prince of Wales.
- 1305 – Wallace is executed in London.
- 1306 – Robert Bruce becomes King of Scots.

Edward II (1284-1327) King of England and Wales. Reigned from 1307 to 1327. The only surviving son of EDWARD I and Eleanor of Castile, he was born at Caernarvon Castle and became the first English Prince of Wales. He succeeded his father in 1307, and was crowned at Westminster Abbey the same year. He was of a mild disposition, but indolent and fond of pleasure. With little contact with his father and surrounded by sisters, he became very reliant on his friends and fiercely loyal to them, regardless of court or public opinion. As king, this weakness for personal favourites Piers Gaveston and, later, Hugh le Despenser, father and son, infuriated the powerful nobles of the land. By the Ordinances of 1311 the barons forced Edward to banish Gaveston and executed him as a public enemy when he disobeyed and returned for the second time.

Two years after this Edward assembled an immense army to check the progress of ROBERT I in Scotland who had been threatening an invasion of England. With superior tactical awareness, Bruce routed the assembled feudal forces of Edward at Bannockburn, near Stirling Castle. Barely escaping the field with his life, it soon became apparent to Edward that his father's plans for a united kingdom stood little chance of success.

Over the next few years his problems extended from France, where his Duchy of Aquataine was overrun by French soldiers, to Ireland, where Bruce had devastated the countryside and threatened the prosperity of the English of the Pale. By 1320 the king also had two new favourites, Sir Hugh Despenser and his son Hugh. Their influence over the king provoked a rebellion by the barons led by the powerful Earl of Lancaster which was defeated at Boroughbridge in Yorkshire. Finally, in 1326 the exiled baron Roger Mortimer invaded England with his mistress, Edward's estranged wife Isabella, to seize power. Their army was completely successful and Edward was deposed. The Despensers, father and son, were captured and executed. Edward was imprisoned in Kenilworth, and then Berkeley Castle in Gloucestershire, and eventually murdered on the or-

ders of Isabella and Mortimer. His death was particularly gruesome as the order for his execution stipu-
lated that no external marks should be left which
would betray violence. The only way to do this was
by disembowelment with a red hot iron inserted into
the rectum, a conventional form of death for homo-
sexuals at the time.

He had four children by Isabella and his son,
EDWARD, became king after him.. He was buried at
Gloucester Cathedral.

Significant events of Edward II's reign

- 1308 – Piers Gaveston is exiled.
- 1312 – Gaveston returns and is put to death.
- 1314 – Edward is defeated by Robert the
  Bruce at Bannockburn.
- 1320 – Sir Hugh Despenser and his son receive
  the favour of the king.
- 1322 – The Baron's revolt is defeated at
  Boroughbridge.
- 1326 – Isabella and Mortimer depose the king.
  The Despensers are executed.

Edward III (1312-1377) King of England and Wales.
Reigned from 1327 to 1377. The eldest son of
EDWARD II and Isabella of France, he was born at
Windsor Castle and succeeded to the throne at the
age of four. During his minority, a council was
elected to govern but his mother's lover, Roger
Mortimer, possessed the principal power in the State.
The pride and oppression of Mortimer led to a gen-

eral confederacy against him, and to his seizure and execution in 1330. Isabella received a yearly pension and quietly retired from public life.

After many years of domestic squabbles, Edward was finally in a position to improve England's international standing. First he turned his attention to Scotland. His claimant for the Scottish throne, EDWARD BALLIOL, the son of JOHN BALLIOL, defeated DAVID II's army and seized the throne, forcing the Scots king into exile. A Scots army then took Balliol by surprise at Annan in Dumfries and expelled him over the border. Edward, having levied a well-appointed army, invaded Scotland and defeated David II's Regent, Donald, at Halidon Hill. This victory produced the restoration of Edward Balliol, who was, however, again expelled.

The ambition of the English king was diverted from Scotland by the prospect of succeeding to the throne of France. To this end Edward initiated the Hundred Years' War in 1337 which was to last intermittently until 1453. Collecting an army and accompanied by his son, the Black Prince, he crossed over to France. There he devastated the northern and eastern territories and declared himself King of France. Memorable victories followed in the Battle of Sluys, in the Battle of Crecy and at the siege of Calais. In the meantime David II, having recovered the throne of Scotland in 1346, invaded England with a large army. The campaign was a disaster, however, and he was defeated and taken prisoner at Neville's Cross, near Durham, by a much inferior force.

In 1348 a truce was concluded with France; but on the death of King Philip, in 1350, Edward again invaded France, plundering and devastating. Recalled home by a Scottish inroad, he retaliated by carrying fire and sword from Berwick to Edinburgh. In the meantime the Black Prince had penetrated from Guienne to the heart of France, fought the famous battle of Poitiers, and taken King John II prisoner. A truce was then made, The Treaty of Brétigny, which gave Edward possession of Calais, Guienne, Gascony and Poitou in return for giving up his claim to the throne. When King John died however, and Charles V became king of France, the two countries resumed hostilities. Edward again crossed over to France and laid waste the provinces of Picardy and Champagne, but at length consented to a peace. This confirmed him in the possession of several provinces and districts of France which were entrusted to the Prince of Wales (the Black Prince), but gradually all the English possessions in France, with the exception of Bordeaux, Bayonne, and Calais, were lost.

The Black Prince died in 1376 and Edward, suffering in his later years from senile dementia, died the following year. He had 13 children by Philippa of Hainault.

Significant events of Edward III's reign

- 1330 – Mortimer is put to death.
- 1332 – Parliament is divided into the two Houses of Lords and Commons for the first time.
- 1333 – David II defeated at Halidon Hill.

- 1337 – The Hundred Years' War commences.
- 1340 – French navy is defeated at Battle of Sluys.
- 1346 – David II is captured at Neville's Cross.
- 1346 – The French are routed at the Battle of Crecy.
- 1347 – Calais is taken by England.
- 1349 – The Black Death reaches England.
- 1356 – The French are defeated at Poitiers.
- 1357 – David II is released from captivity.
- 1362 – English replaces French as the official language of government and the courts.
- 1366 – The Statute of Kilkenny imposes English law in Ireland.
- 1376 – The Black Prince dies.

Edward IV (1442-1483) King of England and Wales. Reigned from 1461 to 1483. The son of Richard Plantagenet, Duke of York, and grandson of Edmund, Earl of Cambridge and Duke of York, fourth son of EDWARD III, he became the first Yorkist king after ousting HENRY VI in the dynastic civil wars later called the Wars of the Roses. The rival line of Lancaster descended from John of Gaunt, the third son of Edward III. The York line had intermarried with the female descendants of Lionel, the second son, which gave it the preferable right to the Crown. Before reaching his twenties Edward led an army against the Lancastrian supporters of Henry VI and defeated them at the Battle of Mortimer's Cross. This avenged the death of his father 'the Protector' Richard, Duke of York, a claimant to the throne. He was then proclaimed king by his cousin Warwick 'the King-maker' and drove Henry north. Edward owed Warwick his crown, however, and hostility soon began to develop between them; Edward had allowed Warwick to govern the kingdom but his marriage to Elizabeth Woodville, the widow of a commoner and daughter of Sir Richard Neville, caused a rift as Warwick felt his position to be threatened. Warwick rebelled against his king, defeated him at Edgecote and left England after a brief period of reconciliation. On his return he allied with the wife of Henry VI, Margaret, to restore the deposed king. Their army caused Edward to flee the realm but he returned the following year to defeat and kill Warwick at the Battle of Barnet. Margaret was also soon defeated at the Battle of Tewkesbury and her son, Edward, was captured and killed. Henry VI was held in the Tower of London where he was later murdered on Edward's orders.

Once he was restored, Edward secured his throne from any further Lancastrian attack by quashing rebellions in the north and began to prove himself as an able ruler in his own right. He set about improving the royal finances which had suffered greatly under Henry VI (he was the first monarch to be solvent at his death for over three hundred years) and establishing good trading relationships abroad. He endeavoured to keep his country out of foreign entanglements and after a short campaign in France withdrew with payments. Recognising the value of wool and cloth, he worked hard to improve trade with German cities and England enjoyed a period of much greater prosperity in the second half of his reign than it had in the first. Law enforcement was similarly improved and he won the respect of his commoners by establishing the Court of Requests which heard complaints against greedy landlords.

The dynastic disputes were not completely forgotten however, and as the Lancastrians were no longer a threat, York turned against York. Edward's two younger brothers, the Dukes of Gloucester and Clarence, both had their eyes set on the throne and Clarence, who had at one time allied himself with the Lancastrians, was accused of treason. He was sent to the Tower where he was later found murdered. After Edward's death Gloucester claimed the throne and had himself crowned as RICHARD III.

Edward had ten children by Elizabeth Woodville and was succeeded by EDWARD V, who, along with his brother Richard, was declared to be illegitimate and deprived of the throne.

Significant events of Edward IV's reign

- 1461 – Edward defeats the Lancastrians at Mortimer's Cross.
- 1464 – Edward is married to Elizabeth Woodville.
- 1469 – Warwick deposes Edward.
- 1470 – Henry VI regains the crown.
- 1471 – Edward restored.

- 1476 – William Caxton brings the printing trade to England.
- 1471 – Duke of Clarence murdered in the Tower.

Edward V (1470-1483) King of England and Wales. Reigned for 77 days in 1483. The eldest son of EDWARD IV and Elizabeth Woodville, he became Prince of Wales in 1471 and was in his thirteenth year when he succeeded his father. Within weeks of becoming king he fell victim to an uncle's ambitions. Richard of Gloucester had been appointed by his dying brother, Edward IV, as Protector of the kingdom during his heir's minority. He had resented the king's marriage to Elizabeth Woodville however, and sought to become king himself. The young prince had been brought up with his brother, Richard, under the power of the Woodville family at Ludlow Castle on the Welsh border. Suspecting that the Woodvilles would remove him from his office as Protector, Gloucester ordered that the senior members be arrested; Edward's grandfather, Earl Rivers and an uncle were killed and his mother forced to seek shelter in Westminster Abbey. Gloucester then placed Edward and his younger brother in the Tower of London, which at that time was a royal residence as well as a prison.

Before the coronation could take place Gloucester declared that the two princes were illegitimate. He had been informed by the Bishop of Bath and Wells that when Edward IV had married their mother he had been betrothed to Lady Eleanor Butler. A betrothal constituted the same commitment as marriage, and consequently Edward IV's marriage was declared void and his sons illegitimate. Parliament had little choice but to agree, and soon after Edward should have been crowned, Gloucester was proclaimed king and took the title RICHARD III.

Edward and Richard vanished, and although no evidence has ever been found, they were undoubtedly murdered in the Tower. Two skeletons were found in 1674 and given a full forensic examination in 1933, but their identity has never been properly established. They were most probably killed by Richard's close associate, Henry Stafford, the Duke of Buckingham, or by Henry Tudor, 2nd Earl of Richmond.

Edward VI (1537-1553) King of England and Ireland. Reigned from 1547 to 1553. The only son of HENRY VIII by Jane Seymour, was born at Hampton Court Palace and on his father's death was only nine years of age. He was too young to shape government and during his minority this was done by two Protectors; firstly Edward Seymour, Duke of Somerset, and then John Dudley, Duke of Northumberland. He grew up with a rooted zeal for the doctrines of the Reformation and made the Catholic mass illegal by the Act of Uniformity in 1549. He also ordered that icons and statues of saints be removed and destroyed and that church walls be whitewashed to cover up paintings. Objections to his reforms led to widespread disquiet and in Devon and Cornwall to a revolt which was put down with severity. His reign also produced the first

Book of Common Prayer written by Thomas Cranmer, the Archbishop of Canterbury, and the later named Thirty-Nine Articles of Religion.

His reign was, on the whole, tumultuous and unsettled. In an attempt to secure Scotland an English army invaded and defeated the Scots at the Battle of Pinkie. Despite this victory, the 'Rough Wooing', as the attempt to marry Mary, Queen of Scots, was later called, failed. In 1551 the Protector Somerset, who had hitherto governed the kingdom with energy and ability, was deposed by the intrigues of Dudley, Duke of Northumberland, who became all-powerful. Somerset was executed two years later. At the end of 1552 Edward contracted tuberculosis of which he would die the following year. Dudley induced the dying Edward to set aside the succession of his sisters, MARY and ELIZABETH, and settle the crown upon LADY JANE GREY, to whom he had married his son Lord Guildford Dudley. The king died, aged 15, at Greenwich Palace in 1553 and Lady Jane was proclaimed Queen, though her reign was to be very brief.

Significant events of Edward VI's reign

- 1547 – The Duke of Somerset is appointed Protector of England.

    Scots defeated at The Battle of Pinkie.

- 1549 – The First Act of Uniformity passed.

- 1550 – John Dudley deposes the Duke of Somerset and becomes Protector.

- 1553 – Lady Jane Grey named as successor to the throne.

Edward VII (1841-1910) King of the United Kingdom
of Great Britain and Ireland and British Dominions
overseas; Emperor of India. Reigned from 1901 to
1910. The eldest son of Queen VICTORIA and the
Prince Albert of Saxe-Coburg-Gotha was born at
Buckingham Palace and created Prince of Wales in
1841. He was educated under private tutors and at
Edinburgh, Oxford, and Cambridge; visited Canada
and the United States in 1860; and underwent military training at the Curragh camp in 1861. Promoted
to the rank of general in 1862, he visited Palestine
and the East, and next year took his seat in the House
of Lords. In 1863 he was married in St George's
Chapel, Windsor Castle, to Princess Alexandra, eldest daughter of Christian IX of Denmark, and from
this time onwards he discharged many public ceremonial functions. Many of these duties he under-
took in the place of Victoria who felt she could not
trust him with domestic political affairs. This
strained relationship meant that he was not given access to any state papers, cabinet reports or diplomatic
correspondence. Excluded from his mother's circle
of advisors, he became more frequently seen at society events, and, although he appeared to remain happily married, it was known that he had many affairs
with actresses and society beauties (he had 13 known
mistresses). As well as a socialite, he was a keen
sportsman and enjoyed gambling, shooting and
yachting. He also took a keen interest in horse-racing
(he owned one Grand National and three Derby win-
ners), motor cars (all his cars displayed the royal

coat-of-arms on the sides), and theatre, which benefited greatly from his patronage. He also had a very strong attachment to France, which, while he was Prince of Wales, very much annoyed his mother who preferred Prussia. By the end of Victoria's reign the diplomatic relationship with France was strained by territorial disputes. Soon after becoming king, however, Edward met the French President, Emile Loubert, in an effort to improve relations. This friendly meeting laid the foundation of the *Entente Cordiale* of the following year which settled many of the old disputes.

He succeeded to the throne on the death of Victoria in 1901 and was crowned the following year at the age of 59. A well-loved king, Edward did much to popularise the monarchy in his nine-year reign. His love of foreign travel and public ceremonial established a more ambassadorial style of monarchy which came to replace the traditional political role of the head of state. His death from bronchitis in 1910 was felt keenly by all strata of society.

Significant events of Edward VII's reign

- 1901 – Australia is granted Dominion status.
- 1902 – The Order of Merit is created by Edward.
- 1903 – The first flight is made by Wilbur and Orville.

  The Women's Social and Political Union is formed by Emmeline Pankhurst.
- 1904 – *Entente Cordial* is reached between Britain and France.

- 1907 – *Entente Cordial* reached between Russia and Britain.

- 1908 – The 4th Olympic Games are held in London.

    Triple Entente is reached between Britain, France and Russia.

- 1909 – Old age pensions introduced.

    Parliament Bill introduced to curb the power of the House of Lords.

Edward VIII (1894-1972) King of Great Britain and Ireland and British Dominions overseas; Emperor of India. Reigned for 325 days (uncrowned). The son of George, Duke of York (GEORGE V) and Princess Mary of Teck. He was educated in England and France and joined the army on the outbreak of war. When it was over he made several extended tours of Europe. He was popular with the public for his great charm and concern for the plight of the unemployed during the recession. Ceremonial duties bored him however, and he was notoriously bad at keeping appointments. His private life met with the disapproval of his father and before his coronation he made it clear he intended to marry Mrs Wallis Simpson, an American who in 1935 was embarking on her second divorce. This was opposed by the Archbishop of Canterbury and the Prime Minister, Baldwin, who held a similar opinion of Edward's private life to Edward's father. Rather than force a constitutional crisis the King decided to abdicate. Edward and Mrs Simpson were created Duke and Duchess of Windsor when they married at Chateau Conde, near Tours, in 1937 and, apart from the war years when he served as Governor of the Bahamas, they lived in France. He remained on good terms with his royal relatives but Mrs Simpson was never accepted. The Duke died in 1972; the Duchess in 1986. They had no children.

Edwin (d.633) King of Northumberland. Reigned from 616 to 633. The heir to the kingdom of Bernicia, he formed an alliance with King REDWALD of East Anglia on his return from exile and defeated his rival, King ETHELFRITH, in battle on the River Idle. He became *Bretwalda*, overlord of all Anglo-Saxon kings. The Northumbrian king married Ethelburga, daughter of Ethelfrith in 625 and embraced Christianity, being baptized at York in 627. He was finally defeated in 633 at Hatfield Chase by an alliance of the Welsh and the Mercians, under King PENDA. The city of Edinburgh derives its name from being Edwin's northern outpost.

Edwy (940-959) King of England. Reigned from 955 to 959. The eldest son of EDMUND I and Elfgifu, he succeeded his uncle EDRED to the throne in 955 at the age of fifteen. He promptly earned himself a reputation as a corrupt and incompetent ruler by leaving the coronation feast with two women. It is said that he was dragged from his bedchamber by Dunstan, the Abbot of Glastonbury, and forced to return to the table. Edwy later exiled the him for his pains. His unpopularity led to the Northumbrians and Mercians to renounce their allegiance to Edwy in favour of his brother, EDGAR, in 557. From then on he ruled only over the area south of the Thames.

Egbert I (d.873) King of Bernicia. Installed as ruler of this kingdom in Northumbria by the Vikings in 867.

Egbert II (d.878) King of Bernicia. Reigned from 876 to 878. The last of the Viking-installed rulers.

Egbert I King of Kent. Reigned from 664 to 673. He extended his kingdom to include Surrey.

Egbert II King of Kent. Reigned from 765 to 780. Failed to win independence from the Mercian over-lords at the Battle of Otford in 766.

Egbert (Egbert III of Kent) (775-839) King of Wessex. Reigned from 802 to 839. His early years were spent in exile at the court of Charlemagne. As king of Wessex (802–39) he defeated BEORNWULF of Mercia and was recognized by Northumbria in 829 as *Bretwalda*, or overall ruler of all Anglo-Saxon kings in England. He made Wessex the leading kingdom in the land and laid the basis for future unification. Under King WIGLAF however, Mercia re-established independence in 830 and thereafter Egbert was effective ruler of Wessex only and its dependant kingdoms of Surrey, Sussex, Kent and Essex.

Egfrith (d.796) King of Mercia. Reigned from 787 to 796. The son of the powerful OFFA, he only survived his father 141 days having ruled jointly with him since 787.

Egfrith (d.685) King of Northumbria. Reigned from

670 to 685. The son of Oswy and Eanfled of Deira. On succeeding to the throne he consolidated his kingdom by driving the Mercians back across the Humber. In the north his expansionist policies were strongly resisted by the Picts and in 685 his army was destroyed at Nechtansmere, near Forfar in Angus. He was killed in the battle.

Egric (d.637) King of East Anglia. Reigned from 634 to 637. A kinsman who took the throne when Sigebert received the tonsure and entered a monastery. He was killed fighting Penda during a Mercian invasion.

Elfward (d.924) King of Wessex. Reigned in 924. An illegitimate son of Edward the Elder, his reign lasted only a few months. His half-brother Ethelstan succeeded him.

Elfwold (d.788) King of Northumbria. Reigned from 779 to 788. The grandson of King Edbert, he deposed Ethelred to take the throne. He was murdered by a supporter of the rival dynasty and buried in Hexham church.

Elhred King of Northumbria. Reigned from 765 to 774. Claiming to belong to the Bernician royal house he deposed Ethelwold Moll in 765. After suffering the same fate and fleeing the kingdom he was succeeded by Ethelred, the son of Ethelwold Moll.

Elizabeth I (1533-1603) Queen of England and Ireland. Reigned from 1558 to 1603. The only child of Henry VIII and Anne Boleyn, she was born at Green-

wich Palace and almost immediately declared heiress
to the crown. After her mother had been beheaded
(1536) both she and her half-sister MARY were declared illegitimate, and she was finally placed after
her half-brother, EDWARD, and the Lady Mary in the
order of succession. On the accession of Edward VI
Elizabeth was committed to the care of the Queen-
Dowager Catherine; and after the death of Catherine
and execution of her consort Thomas Seymour she
was closely watched at Hatfield, where she received
a classical education under William Grindal and
Roger Ascham.

At the death of Edward, Elizabeth vigorously supported the title of Mary against the pretensions of
LADY JANE GREY, but continued throughout the whole
reign to be an object of suspicion and surveillance. In
self-defence she made every demonstration of zeal-
ous adherence to the Roman Catholic faith, but her
inclinations were well known. When Mary died
Elizabeth was immediately recognized as queen by
Parliament. The accuracy of her judgement showed
itself in her choice of advisers, Parker, a moderate divine (Archbishop of Canterbury 1559), aiding her in
ecclesiastical policy; while William Cecil assisted
her in foreign affairs. The first great object of her
reign was the settlement of religion, to effect which a
Parliament was called on 25th January, and dissolved
on the 8th of May, its object having been accom-
plished. The nation was prepared for a return to the
Reformed faith, and Parliament was at the bidding of
the Court. The ecclesiastical system devised in her

father's reign was re-established, the royal supremacy asserted, and the revised Prayer Book enforced by the Act of Uniformity. While, however, the formal establishment of the reformed religion was easily completed, the security and defence of the settlement was the main object of the policy and the chief source of all the struggles and contentions of her reign. Freed from the tyranny of Mary's reign, the Puritans began to claim predominance for their own dogmas, while the supporters of the Established Church were unwilling to grant them even liberty of worship. The Puritans, therefore, like the Catholics, became irreconcilable enemies of the existing order, and increasingly stringent measures were adopted against them. But the struggle against the Catholics was the more severe, chiefly because they were supported by foreign powers; so that while their religion was wholly prohibited, even exile was forbidden them, in order to prevent their intrigues abroad. Many Catholics, particularly priests, suffered death during her reign; but simple nonconformity, from whatever cause, was pursued with the severest penalties, and many more clergymen were driven out of the Church, by differences about the position of altars, the wearing of caps, and such like matters, than were forced to resign by the change from Rome to Reformation.

Elizabeth's first Parliament approached her on a subject which, next to religion, was the chief trouble of her reign, the succession to the Crown. They requested her to marry, but she declared her intention

to live and die a virgin; and she consistently declined
in the course of her life such suitors as the Duke
d'Alençon, Prince Erik of Sweden, the Archduke
Charles of Austria, and Philip of Spain, while, however, she felt that she could best maintain her power
by remaining unmarried, she knew how to temporize
with suitors for political ends, and showed the greatest
jealousy of all pretenders to the English succession.

With the unfortunate MARY, Queen of Scots were
connected many of the political events of Elizabeth's
reign. On her accession the country was at war with
France. Peace was easily concluded (1559); but the
assumption by Francis and Mary of the royal arms
and titles of England led to an immediate interfer-
ence on the part of Elizabeth in the affairs of Scotland. She entered into a league with the Lords of the
Congregation, or leaders of the Reformed party; and
throughout her reign this party was frequently serv-
iceable in furthering her policy. She also gave early
support to the Huguenot party in France, and to the
Protestants in the Netherlands, so that throughout
Europe she was looked on as the head of the Protestant party. This policy roused the implacable resentment of Philip, who strove in turn to excite the
Catholics against her both in her own dominions and
in Scotland. The detention of Mary in England
(1568-87), where she fled to the protection of Elizabeth, led to a series of conspiracies, beginning with
that under the Earls of Northumberland and
Westmoreland, and ending with the plot of
Babington, which finally forced the reluctant Eliza-

beth to order her execution. Mary's death (1587), though it has stained her name to posterity, tended to confirm her power among her contemporaries. The state of France consequent on the accession of Henry IV, who was assisted by Elizabeth, obviated any danger from the indignation which the execution had caused in that country; and the awe in which King James stood of Elizabeth and his dread of interfering with his own right of succession to England made him powerless.

Philip of Spain was not to be so appeased, the execution of Mary lending edge to other grievances. The fleets of Elizabeth had galled him in the West Indies and her arms and subsidies had helped to deprive him of the Netherlands. Soon his Armada was prepared, ready to sail for England. Accordingly he called the Queen of England a murderess, and refused to be satisfied even with the sacrifice she seemed prepared to make of her Dutch allies. The Armada sailed in 1588 but the great naval force was broken up by English fireships and sent in retreat up the east coast and round the rocky shoreline of northern Scotland. It is not known how many of the ships returned to Spain, but at least one-third of the crews, 11,000 men, were lost at sea. The war with Spain dragged on till the close of Elizabeth's long reign.

During her reign the splendour of her government at home and abroad was sustained by such men as Cecil, Bacon, Walshingham, and Throgmorton; but she had personal favourites of less merit who were

often more brilliantly rewarded. Chief of these were
Dudley, whom she created Earl of Leicester, and
whom she was disposed to marry, and Essex, whose
violent passions brought about his ruin when he rebelled against the government. He was beheaded in
1601; but Elizabeth never forgave herself his death.
She died two years later of blood poisoning from a
tonsillar abscess, having named JAMES VI of Scotland
as her successor.

Significant events of Elizabeth I's reign

- 1558 – Cecil appointed Chief Secretary of State.
- 1559 – Matthew Parker appointed Archbishop of
Canterbury.
Elizabeth becomes head of the English
Church via the Act of Supremacy.
- 1560 – Treaty of Berwick promises Scottish
Protestants English aid against French.

    William Cecil appointed Chief Secretary
of State.
- 1563 – 15,000 die in the Plague of London.
- 1568 – Mary, Queen of Scots, is imprisoned by
Elizabeth.
- 1580 – Francis Drake returns to England having
circumnavigated the world.
- 1586 – Mary, Queen of Scots, stands trial for
treason
- 1587 – Mary, Queen of Scots, is executed.
- 1588 – The Spanish Armada is destroyed.
- 1601 – Earl of Essex is executed.

Elizabeth II (1926-) Queen of the United Kingdom of
Great Britain and Northern Ireland and other realms
and territories; Head of the Commonwealth and
Head of State for sixteen of its members. The present
queen was born at 17 Brunton Street, London, the
eldest daughter of King GEORGE VI and Lady Elizabeth Bowes-Lyon. She was privately educated and at
the outbreak of World War Two, under the threat of
bombing, the princess and her sister Margaret were
moved from London to Windsor Castle (Buckingham Palace was bombed on 12 September 1940). As
a girl she had no expectations of becoming queen,
but the abdication of EDWARD VIII meant her father
reluctantly became George VI. In 1944 at the age of
18 she trained with the Auxiliary Transport Service,
becoming a capable driver. She married in 1947 to
Philip Mountbatten (son of Prince Andrew of Greece
and made Duke of Edinburgh on his marriage) and
has four children; Charles, born 14th November
1948 (made Prince of Wales in 1969), Anne, born
15th August 1950 (made Princess Royal in 1987),
Andrew, born 19th February 1960 (later to become
Duke of York), and Edward, born 10th March 1964.
Elizabeth acceded to the throne on the death of her
father on 6 February 1952 (whilst on tour in Africa)
aged 25 and was crowned at Westminster Abbey on
the 2nd of June 1953.

The Queen's full title in the United Kingdom is:
'Elizabeth the Second, by the Grace of God, of the
United Kingdom of Great Britain and Northern Ire-
land and of Her other Realms and Territories Queen,

Head of the Commonwealth, Defender of the Faith'. Her right to this title derives from the common-law rules of heredity and from legislation such as the Act of Settlement made in 1700 which states that only Protestant descendants of Electress Sophia of Hanover, granddaughter of JAMES I, may succeed to the throne. The succession can only be changed if all the members of the Commonwealth which recognize the Queen as sovereign consent to the change. Only if this happens can someone other than the eldest son of the sovereign succeed to the throne.

As head of state of one of the last remaining constitutional monarchies, Queen Elizabeth's duties include the opening of Parliament and, as commander of the British armed forces, the inspection of the Trooping of the Colour. She also has the authority to pardon criminals, appoint government ministers and judges, and as Head of the Church of England it is she who appoints bishops. All these decisions are made however, only with the advice of her government. In her long reign she has seen several Prime Ministers come and go and all cabinet papers pass before her, as does all important diplomatic correspondence. She also sees the Prime Minister once a week and gives advice on government affairs which is rarely ignored.

A hard working ambassador for the United Kingdom, the Queen has made state visits worldwide, a feature of these being her informal 'walkabouts' which enable her to have direct contact with her public. During her reign she has done much to bring the monarchy closer to the people but as a result she and her family have been subject to almost constant invasions of privacy by the world's media. The strain of being the most photographed family in the world has taken its toll on the relationships and marriages of the younger Windsors.

Significant events of the reign

- 1955 – Churchill resigns as Prime Minister and Anthony Eden takes his place.

  Nationalization of the Suez Canal.

- 1957 – Macmillan becomes Prime Minister.

- 1960 – Nigeria and Cyprus gain independence.

- 1963 – Macmillan government collapses.

- 1964 – Harold Wilson becomes Prime Minister.

  Cunard liner *Queen Elizabeth II* is launched.

- 1969 – Charles invested as Prince of Wales.

  British troops deployed in Ulster to control sectarian disturbances.

- 1970 – Edward Heath becomes Prime Minister

- 1973 – Britain joins the European Community.

- 1974 – Harold Wilson returns as Prime Minister.

- 1979 – Margaret Thatcher becomes first woman Prime Minister.

- 1980 – Rhodesia gains independence as Zimbabwe.

- 1981 – Prince Charles marries Lady Diana Spencer.

- 1982 – Britain goes to war with Argentina over control of the Falkland Islands.
- 1990 – Rioters in London protest against the Poll Tax.
- 1991 – Gulf War threatens Middle East relations.
- 1992 – Windsor Castle damaged by fire.

    Charles and Diana announce separation

- 1993 – The Queen agrees to pay tax on private income.
- 1994 – The Queen visits Russia.
- 1993 – The Queen visits South Africa.

Enfrith (d.633) King of Bernicia. Reigned in 633. The eldest son of ETHELFRITH, he married a Pictish princess but was killed after reigning for less than a year by the Welsh king, CADWALLON, at a battle near Doncaster.

Enred (d.c.841) King of Northumbria. Reigned from 809 to c.841. A son of EARDWULF, he succeeded his father in 809 and in 829 made a formal submission to EGBERT of Wessex. He maintained his kingdom without recorded incident for more than thirty years.

Eocha (d.889) King of Scots. Reigned from 878 to 889. The son of RUN, King of Strathclyde, and grandson of KENNETH mac-Alpin. He ruled jointly with his cousin, GIRIC I, the son of DONALD I, before being deposed.

Eochaid I (the Yellow-Haired) (d.c.629) King of Scots. The son and successor of AIDEN.

Eochaid II (d.*c*.679) King of Scots. Also known as 'Eochaid the Crook-Nose'.

Eochaid III (d.*c*.733) King of Scots. The last to rule in Irish Dalriada.

Eochaid IV (the Venomous) (d.*c*.737) King of Scots. Reigned between 733 and 737. He married a Pictish princess and his son, ALPIN, was the father of KENNETH MAC-ALPIN who became the first king of the Dalriadic Scots and the Picts.

Eormenric (d.*c*.560) King of Kent. Reigned from *c*.540 to 560. A son of AESC.

Eorpwold (d.627) King of East Anglia. Reigned from *c*.617 to 627. A son of REDWALD, he was converted to Christianity by EDWIN of Northumbria and murdered by a rival to the throne.

Eppilus (*c*.AD 15) King of the Atrebates tribe. One of the three sons of COMMIUS who divided his kingdom and used the Roman title *Rex* meaning 'king'.

Erconbert (d.664) King of Kent. Reigned from c660 to 664. He married Sexburga, one of King ANNA of East Anglia's four daughters.

Eric (d.918) King of East Anglia. Reigned from 900 to 902. He succeeded his father, GUTHRUM, and was killed fighting EDWARD the Elder's army. He was the last Dane to rule the kingdom of East Anglia.

Erik Bloodaxe (d.954) King of York. Reigned from 947 to 954. After being deposed as King of Norway in 934 he fled to England and seized Northumbria from EDRED in 947. He was killed along with his brother and a son in an ambush at Stainmore by Edred's army

Ethelbald (d.757) King of Mercia. Reigned from 716 to 757. By 731 Ethelbald had established himself as *Bretwada*, or overlord, of all the kingdoms south of the Humber and styled himself *Rex Britanniae*, King of Britain. He was nonetheless troubled by frequent Welsh raids and had the fortifications of Wat's Dyke built as a bulwark against aggression. He was murdered by his bodyguard in 757 and is buried at Repton, Derbyshire.

Ethelbald (834-860) King of Wessex. Reigned from 858 to 860. He ascended the throne on the death of his father ETHELWULF, but reigned for only two years. He married his stepmother Judith. He is buried at Sherborne Abbey, Dorset.

Ethelbert I (d.616) King of Kent. Reigned from 560 to 616. Ruler of all England south of the Humber, he married Bertha, daughter of the Frankish King Charibert, *c.*589. He became the first baptized Anglo-Saxon king after receiving St Augustine's mission from Rome in 597 which landed at Ebbsfleet, near Ramsgate. He made Canterbury the centre of Christianity in southern England and is buried there in the Monastery of St Peter and St Paul. He was succeeded by EDBALD who temporarily renounced Christianity and married his stepmother.

Ethelbert II (d.762) King of Kent. Reigned from 725 to 762. The son of WIHTRED and Cynegyth, he reigned jointly to 748 with his brother, EADBERT, and then with his half-brothers, ALRIC and EARDWULF.

Ethelbert (St Ethelbert) (d.792) King of East Anglia. Reigned in 792. He was executed by his father-in-law, King OFFA of Mercia, and is the patron saint of Hereford Cathedral.

Ethelbert (836-865) King of Wessex. Reigned from 857 to 865. The third son of ETHELWULF, succeeded his elder brother ETHELSTAN in the Eastern side of the kingdom in 857, and in 860, on the death of his brother, ETHELBALD, became sole king. He was troubled by the inroads of the Danes who sacked Kent and crushed Winchester during his reign. He was buried at Sherborne Abbey in Dorset.

Ethelfrith (d.617) King of Northumbria. Reigned from 604 to 617. The third of IDA's six sons, he reigned in Bernicia from 592 and seized Deira in 604. In his efforts to expand his realm he defeated King AIDEN of the Dalriadic Scots at Degastan, near Liddesdale, in 603. He also took Chester from the Welsh in 613. He married three times and had seven sons and three daughters.

Ethelheard (d.740) King of Wessex. Reigned from 726 to c740. Succeeded INE as king in 726 although his connection to him is unknown. A land charter he made to Bishop Fortherne in 739 first mentions Devon.

Ethelhere (d.654) King of East Anglia. Reigned in

654. A younger brother of ANNA, he reigned for only a few months before being killed in the Battle of Winwaed fighting the South Saxons with PENDA of Mercia.

Ethelred King of Mercia. Reigned from 675 to 704. A brother of WULFHERE, he abdicated to become a monk.

Ethelred I (d.796) King of Northumbria. Reigned from 774 to 796. The son of ETHELWOLD MOLL, he deposed ELHRED, who had deposed his father, in 774. He earned a reputation as a tyrant after having several of his nobles executed for treachery and was briefly deposed by ELFWOLD, the grandson of King EDBERT. He returned to the throne in 790 after imprisoning OSRED, nephew of Elfwold. Osred later escaped and Ethelred was murdered at Corbridge by Hadrian's Wall. OSBALD, one of those who conspired against him, took the throne.

Ethelred II King of Northumbria. Reigned from 841 to 850. The son of EANRED.

Ethelred I (St Elthelred) (840-871) King of Wessex. Reigned from 865 to 871. The son of ETHELWULF, he succeeded his brother, ETHELBERT, at a time when the Danes were threatening the conquest of the whole kingdom. He died in consequence of a wound received in action with the Danes at the Battle of Merton in 871, and was succeeded by his brother, ALFRED. Ethelred's devout Christianity was recognised in his popular title of St Ethelred.

Ethelred (II) the Unready (968-1016) King of England.

Reigned from 978 to 1016. The son of EDGAR and Emma of Norway, he succeeded his brother, EDWARD the Martyr, and, for his lack of vigour and capacity, earned the name of 'the Unready'. In his reign he began the practice of buying off the Danes by presents of money. After repeated payments of tribute (known as 'dane-geld'), he effected, in 1002, a massacre of the Danes; but this led to SWEYN gathering a large force together and ravaging the country. They were again bribed to depart; but upon a new invasion, Sweyn obliged the nobles to swear allegiance to him as king of England. Ethelred fled to Normandy but returned after the death of Sweyn in 1004 when he was invited to resume the government. He died in London in the midst of a struggle with CANUTE, his Danish rival for the throne. He married twice and among his children were EDMUND II and EDWARD the Confessor. His second marriage to the daughter of the 2nd Duke of Normandy formed an Anglo-Norman connection which provided a basis for the Norman invasion of 1066.

Ethelric King of Bernicia. Reigned from 568 to 572. A son of the Saxon king IDA, Ethelric ruled Bernicia, which, with Deira, ruled by his brother AELLE, later formed the kingdom of Northumbria. Bernicia supplied most of the kings in the merged kingdom.

Ethelstan (895-939) King of England. Reigned from 924 to 939. The eldest son of EDWARD the Elder and Egwina, he was crowned at Kingston-on Thames and became the first Saxon king with effective control of all England (with the exception of Cumbria). He was an able ruler and with the combined forces of Mercia and Wessex was victorious in his wars with the Danes of Northumberland, and with the Scots and Irish, by whom they were assisted, at Brunanburh, an unidentified site in Cumbria, in 937. In this battle a son of the king of Scots and five Irish kings were killed, shattering the Viking-Scots coalition. He also summoned a number of Welsh princes to Hereford and imposed a tribute on them, as well as fixing the border between his kingdom and that of the princes at Wye. He became therefore, in name at least, the overlord of Celtic kingdoms in Cornwall, Scotland, and Wales.

Ethelstan sought to ease the plight of his poorer subjects through some of the many laws he introduced which punished theft and corruption. He established a corps of clerks that is thought to have foreshadowed the civil service, as well introducing a national coinage. He also strengthened relations with continental rulers through the marriages of four of his sisters to dukes in France and Holy Roman Emperor Otto I the Great. He was buried in Malmesbury Abbey in Wiltshire.

Ethelwald (Moll) King of Northumbria. Reigned from 759 to 765. Defeated his rival for the throne, OSWIN, in 761 but was deposed by ELHRED (who claimed to be a descendant of IDA, the founder of the Bernician dynasty) four years later.

Ethelwalh King of Sussex. Reigned before 685. He received the Isle of Wight from WULFERHERE of Mercia in 661 and in turn gave WILFRED the bisopric of Selsey.

Ethelweard King of Mercia. Reigned c.837 to 850.

Ethelwold King of Mercia. Reigned from 654 to 663. The youngest brother of ANNA.

Ethelwulf (800-858) King of Wessex. Reigned from 839 to 858. He succeeded his father, EGBERT, and was chiefly occupied in repelling Danish incursions. He is best remembered for his donation to the clergy, which is often quoted as the origin of the system of tithes. ALFRED the Great was the youngest of his five children.

F

Fergus Mor (d.501) King of Scots. The son of Erc, he was the ruler of the kingdom of Dalriada in Argyll which also included the Inner Hebrides and part of Northern Ireland. He led a group of his people, the 'Scots', from Antrim in northern Ireland to settle in western Scotland around 500 and is credited with introducing the Gaelic language to Scotland, as well as the term 'Scot' from which the country was later to take its name. All kings of Dalriada for the following 343 years claimed descent from either Fergus or Loarn, another son of Erc.

G

Garnard (d.635) King of Picts. Reigned from 631 to 635. The son of CINOICH's sister.

Gartnait (d.663) King of Picts. Reigned from 657 to 663. The son of TALORCEN's sister.

Gartnart (d.597) King of Picts. He reigned *c.*586 to 597. The son of BRIDEI I's sister,

George I (1660-1727) King of Great Britain and Ireland. Reigned from 1714 to 1727. 2nd Elector of Hanover from 1698. The son of the 1st Elector of Hanover, Ernest Augustus, by Sophia, daughter of Frederick, Elector Palatine, and grand-daughter of JAMES I, he inherited the throne through his mother following the Act of Succession of 1701 which conferred the succession on her heirs.

In 1682 he was married to Sophia Dorothea of Zell, whom, in 1694, on account of a suspected intrigue with Count Königsmark, he caused to be imprisoned and kept in confinement for the rest of her life. In 1698 he succeeded his father as the 2nd Elector of Hanover (Electors were princes of the Holy Roman Empire who elected the Emperor). He commanded the imperial army in 1707 during the war of the Spanish Succession; and ascended the throne of Great Britain on the death of Queen ANNE in 1714. He arrived in Britain at the age of 54 and, as he spoke only German, had a very limited knowledge of the kingdom. It was a difficult succession as there were many who wanted the Stuart dynasty to continue and within a year he was faced with a Scottish-led Jacobite rebellion. The attempt to place the 'Old Pretender', JAMES II's son, James Stuart Edward, on the throne was a failure however, as a series of tactical errors led to the Jacobite army being defeated in the Battle of Sherrifmuir.

More than most monarchs, George needed good advisers and men he could trust in government. Sadly the leading men of the day were mostly corrupt and sought to take advantage of a political system which was almost entirely devoid of integrity. The poor character of the nation at large was exposed by the disaster involving the South Sea Company. Thousands invested in this trading company, but in 1720 the South Sea Bubble, as it came to be known, burst. Most of the investors lost their money and the government was engulfed in scandal. A radical change was required in the financial administration of the country and it was only with the appointment of Sir Robert Walpole as First Lord of the Treasury that confidence was restored. For twenty-one years Walpole oversaw the restructuring of government and became, in effect, the first Prime Minister. The king came to depend on him and his Whig ministry, although, because he could not speak English, he could not preside over meetings of Walpole's cabinet.

The private character of George I was bad, but he showed much good sense and prudence in government, especially of his German dominions and was an able military leader. Other than his patronage of Handel, he had little time for the arts and was widely disliked for his treatment of his wife and for his many mistresses. He died of a stroke while visiting his German possessions. By Sophia Dorothea he had a son, George, afterwards GEORGE II of England, and a daughter, Sophia, the mother of Frederick the Great.

Significant events of George I's reign

- 1715 – Jacobites are defeated at Sherrifmuir.
- 1716 – The Septennial Act allows for General Elections to be held every seven years.
- 1720 – The collapse of the South Seas Company.
- 1721 – Sir Robert Walpole becomes the first Prime Minister.
- 1726 – The first British circulating library opens in Edinburgh.

   Daniel Defoe's *Gulliver's Travels* is published.
- 1727 – Sir Issac Newton dies.

George II (1683-1760) King of Great Britain and Ireland. Reigned from 1727 to 1760. The only son of GEORGE I and Sophia Dorothea of Celle. In 1708, then only electoral prince of Hanover, he distin-

guished himself at Oudenrarde under Marlborough. He succeeded his father to the English throne, and inherited to the full the predilection of George I for Hanover. For the first twelve years however, he was well served by Prime Minister Robert Walpole who kept England out of foreign entanglements and their relationship can be said to have laid the foundations of constitutional monarchy.

After 1739 Britain was involved in almost continous warfare; first with Spain, then with France during the War of the Austrian Succession and then again with France during the Seven Years War. The events in Europe led to the resignation of Walpole in 1742, for he was no war minister, and his place was taken for the next twenty years by Henry Pelham and his brother the Duke of Newcastle. With the British army engaged in Flanders the Scottish Jacobites took the opportuinity to attempt again the restoration of a Stuart to the thone. This time it was the 'Young Pretender', Charles Edward Stuart, the son of James Edward Stuart. He landed from France in the Highlands of Scotland and raised an army among the clan chiefs loyal to the Stuarts. The Jacobite army was at first successful, taking Edinburgh with little difficulty and routing an English army at Prestonpans, before advancing south. Support hoped for in the north of England never materialized however, and following a long and tiring retreat, the Jacobites was crushed by the British army, now returned from Flanders, under the command of William, Duke of Cumberland, son of George II, at Culloden. In the aftermath 'Bonny Prince Charlie' escaped to France leaving his Highland supporters to face deportation or execution. Many clan chiefs lost their estates and possessions and the Highlands of Scotland, which had for so long remained distant from royal authority, where at last brought under control.

There was further success for Charles in the victories of the Seven Years War; the year of 1759 saw France lose important territories in North America and their stronghold, Quebec, was taken by General Wolfe; in India Clive defeated the French at Plassey and Madras giving the East India Company control of the vast province of Bengal. By 1763 France had ceded all Canada to Britain and retained only two small trading posts in India; the last years of George's reign saw Britain well on its way to becoming a truly world power.

The reign was also notable for the number of great men in art, letters, war, and diplomacy who then adorned Britain. George II had a keen interest in music and continued his father's patronage of Handel, but was a king of very moderate abilities and ignorant of science or literature. He nevertheless won respect for his military abilities; at Dettingen (1743) he became the last British king to lead his troops into battle. In matters of state he was guided by his wife, Caroline of Ansbach, who was far more cultured and intelligent than her husband. By Caroline he had three sons and four daughters, notably Frederick, Prince of Wales, Anne, William, Duke of Cumberland, Mary and Louisa.

Significant events of George II's reign

- 1732 – A royal charter founds Georgia.
- 1738 – The Methodist movement is founded by John and Charles Wesley.
- 1740 – War of Austrian Sucession begins.
- 1742 – Handel's *Messiah* first performed.
- 1743 – George leads troops at Dettingen.
- 1745 – The Jacobites gain victory at Prestonpans.
- 1746 – The Battle of Culloden crushes the Jacobite rising.
- 1753 – The British Museum is founded.
- 1757 – Robert Clive secures Bengal for Britain.

  William Pitt becomes Prime Minister.
- 1759 – Quebec is taken by James Wolfe.

George III (1738-1820) King of Great Britain and Ireland. Reigned from 1760 to 1820. From 1801 he became King of the United Kingdom of Great Britain and Ireland. 4th Elector of Hanover (*de facto* until 1803). The eldest son of Frederick Louis, Prince of Wales, by the Princess Augusta of Saxe-Coburg-Gotha, he succeeded his grandfather, GEORGE II, in 1760. In the following year he married the Princess Charlotte Sophia of Mecklenburg-Strelitz. The sixty years of his reign are filled with great events, amongst which are the acceleration of the Industrial Revolution; the Wilkes controversy; the American Revolution, 1775-83, the result of which the king felt acutely; the French Revolution, 1789, and the Napoleonic Wars which followed, comprising the long struggle that ended at Waterloo; and the Irish Rebellion of 1798.

He was the first Hanovarian monarch to be raised in England and took a great interest in government, although he was also thought by many to interfere too much. His first Prime Minister, Bute, proved unpopular and failed to please George. He was followed by a succession of ministers who also met with the king's disapproval. In 1770 he appointed Lord North and established a good working relationship which lasted to 1783. After the losses to Britain suffered in the American War of Independence however, North was held responsible, and George also had to shoulder some of the blame. William Pitt the Younger replaced North and guided Britain through the troubled times following the French Revolution. The victories of Waterloo and Trafalgar in the Napoleonic Wars restored some British pride but the death of Nelson, Britain's greatest naval commander, was keenly felt as where the social consequences of twenty-two years of continous war with France.

In Ireland a rebellion in 1798 was followed by Pitt's attempt to solve the Irish problem by passing an Act of Union, similar to that of Scotland one hundred years earlier, whereby Irelnd returned members to the British Parliament. But these members were Protestant as Irish Catholics, although they had the vote, could not sit in Parliament. George denied Pitt's attempts to give them this right and, after the bribing of the Irish Protestants, the assembly in Ireland dissolved itself and the country became governed by a Protestant Parliament of the newly-formed United Kingdom at Westminster.

By this time however, George lost the ability to rule through a disease which had the appearence of a slowly worsening mental illness. It is now though that he had a rare and incurable ailment called porphyria, in which the victim suffers delusions and displays symptoms of delirium. In the last nine years of his life the attacks became more frequent and he died deaf, blind and in a state of permanent derangement.

George III was a man of conscientious principles and of a plain, sound understanding, though his narrow patriotism and his obstinate prejudices were often hurtful to British interests. His tastes and amusements were plain and practical and he enjoyed touring the country. His special interest in agriculture earned him the nickname 'Farmer George'. With Queen Caroline he had fifteen children, nine being sons. His son, GEORGE, had been made Prince Regent in 1811 and succeeded to the throne on his father's death.

Significant events of George III's reign

- 1769 – James Cook begins his first voyage around the world.

- 1773 – The Boston Tea Party sparks protest against unfair British taxation.

- 1774 – The first Continental Congress meets in Philadelphia to protest at the repressive British legislation.

- 1775 – American War of Independence commences.

  The first commercial steam engines are produced by Watt and Boulton.

- 1783 – Britain acknowledges the independence of the American Colonies.

  William Pitt the Younger becomes Prime Minister.

- 1789 – The French Revolution.

- 1791 – First publication of Thomas Paine's *Rights of Man*.

- 1793 – Britain and France go to war.

- 1800 – Act of Union with Ireland.

- 1803 – Napoloenic Wars commence.

- 1805 – Nelson dies in the Battle of Trafalgar.

- 1810 – Prince George, George III's son, becomes Regent.

- 1815 – The Battle of Waterloo ends the Napoleonic Wars.

  The Corn Laws are passed.

- 1819 – The Peterloo Massacre; reform campaigners in Manchester are killed.

George IV (1762-1830) King of the United Kingdom of Great Britain and Ireland. Reigned from 1820 to 1830. The eldest son of GEORGE III and Charlotte Sophia. In 1811 George became Regent and, on the death of his father nine years later, king. He distinguished himself while Regent as a great patron of the arts—the first George about which that could be said—and his intelligent patronage fostered painting, literature and Regency architecture. His extravagant tastes in food and wine were well known, but in the early part of his life these weaknesses did not harm his popularity.

His secret marriage to Maria FitzHerbert, a Catholic, caused problems however, as the 1701 Act of Settlement prohibited the succession of a Catholic to the throne. Forced by Parliament to choose an official wife he married his cousin, Caroline of Brunswick, and had his huge debts paid off in return. The couple soon parted amid accusations of adultery from both sides. George lost his good standing with the people however, when he openly accused his wife of infidelity at a public trial and forbid her from attending his coronation.

The most significant event of his reign was the Catholic Relief Act of 1829 which finally allowed Catholics access to Parliament. There were also important advances made in criminal law and labour relations. George had little interest in politcs however, and spent the majority of his time as king indulging himself with drink, food, and his many mistresses. His dissipated life and his extravagance alienated from him the affection of the nation and the image of the monarchy as a moral influence was greatly tarnished. He died in a state of obesity of internal bleeding and liver damage in 1830. As his only daughter, Princess Charlotte, wife of Leopold of Saxe-Coburg (afterwards King of the Belgians), died childless in 1817, he was succeeded by his brother, WILLIAM IV.

Significant events of George IV's reign

- 1820 –The Cato Street Conspiracy to assassinate the Cabinet is discovered.

  Queen Caroline is tried and George sues for divorce on grounds of adultery.

- 1824 – The National Gallery is founded in London.

- 1825 – The world's first railway service, the Stockton and Darlington Railway, opens.

  Legalisation of Trade Unions.

- 1828 – Wellington becomes Prime Minister.

- 1829 – The establishment of the Metropolitan Police Force by Robert Peel takes place.

  The Catholic Releif Act passed.

George V (1865-1936) King of Great Britain and Ireland and of the overseas British dominions, Emperor of India. Reigned from 1910 to 1936. The second son of EDWARD VII and Queen Alexandra of Denmark. He was born at Marlborough House and after being educated by a private tutor, he and his elder brother, Prince Albert Victor, became naval cadets, and as midshipmen visited many parts of the world. Prince George attained the rank of commander in 1891, but his brother's death in 1892, which placed him in direct succession to the crown, led to his practical withdrawal from a naval career. Created Duke of York in 1892, the following year he married Princess Victoria Mary, daughter of the Duke of Teck. On the death of Queen Victoria and accession of Edward VII he became Duke of Cornwall, and later in the year was created Prince of Wales. On the death of Edward VII the prince became king as George V.

He ascended the throne in the middle of a constitutional crisis caused by the House of Commons attempting to limit the powers of the House of Lords and within four years he was also leading the nation in the First World War. Although he was related to Kaiser Wilhelm II he had no objections to his government's decision to engage Germany in war. He quickly gained the admiration of the public by visiting the troops on the Western Front and openly disapproving of Wilhelm's military gesturing. In 1917 he changed the British royal family's name from the German Saxe-Coburg-Gotha to the English Windsor.

As well as carrying out his royal duties with great conscientiousness, he made important contributions to the handling of political problems of the day. Shortly before the outbreak of the war, he summoned a conference of party leaders at Buckingham Palace for the purpose of solving the Irish question. This was an important step towards the post-war creation of the Irish Free State. Later, during the 1931 financial crisis, he intervened to persuade the leading political parties to form a national coalition government.

On Christmas Day 1932 George broadcast a message to the nation (which had been written by Rudyard Kipling) and established a tradition which has been maintained every year since. His hobbies were shooting and stamp-collecting; his collection is well-known by philatelists. In later life he suffered ill-health and almost died from septicaemia, or blood-poisoning in 1928. He never fully regained his former vigour and died of bronchitis eight years later. He was succeeded by Edward VIII, who abdicated before being coronated, in favour of his brother, George VI.

Significant events of George V's reign

- 1911 – Parliament Act ensures the sovereinty of the House of Commons.

     National Insurance Act passed.

- 1912 – The sinking of the S.S. Titanic.

- 1914 – The First World War breaks out.

- 1916 – The Easter Rising in support of Irish independence takes place in Dublin.

     David Lloyd George becomes Prime Minister.

- 1917 – The Russian Revolution.

- 1918 – Women over thirty gain the vote.

     Irish Parliament formed in Dublin.

- 1919 – The first woman MP, Lady Astor, takes her seat in Parliament.

- 1921 – Ireland partitioned.

- 1924 – First Labour government takes power under Ramsay MacDonald.

- 1926 – A General Strike is called by Trade Unions.

- 1928 – Women over twenty-one get the vote.

George VI (1895-1952) King of the United Kingdom
of Great Britain and Northern Ireland and British dominions overseas; the last Emperor of India; Head of
the Commonwealth from 1949. The second son of
GEORGE V and Queen Mary. Prince Albert, as he was
then known, served in the navy and air force until
1919 and attended trinity College, Cambridge, until
1920. He was called to the throne in 1936 on the abdication of his brother, EDWARD VIII.

Unprepared for the role of king, George nevertheless carried out his duties with great conscientiousness and became a popular figurehead for the nation
during the Second World War. He struggled with a
speech impediment in his early years but worked
hard to overcome it in order to perform his duties
with the sense of authority that he knew was expected of him. He lived in London for the duration of
the war despite frequent bombing raids and visited
the troops in North Africa and France.

In 1939 he became the first British monarch to visit
North America and restored much of the reputation
lost by the monarchy following his brother's abdication. The post-war years saw a Labour government
transforming Britain into a welfare state and George
became Head of the Commonwealth of Nations, following the fragmentation of the Empire.

He opened the 1951 Festival of Britain but died the
next year after an operation for lung cancer. He had
two daughters by Lady Elizabeth-Bowes Lyon (now
the Queen Mother), and was succeeded by the eldest,
the present Queen ELIZABETH.

Significant events of George VI's reign

- 1939 – World War Two breaks out.
- 1940 – The Dunkirk evacuation takes place.

  Winston Churchill becomes Prime Minister.

  The Battle of Britain prevents German invasion.
- 1941 – Pearl Harbour bombing brings the USA into the war.
- 1944 – D-Day; Allied forces land at Normandy and force German retreat.
- 1945 – Germany is defeated and war ends in Europe.

  Japan surrenders and World War Two ends.

  United Nations founded.

  Labour Government elected.
- 1947 – India and Pakistan gain independence.
- 1948 – Establishment of the National Health Service.
- 1951 – Festival of Britain opens.

Giric I (d.889) King of Scots. Reigned from 878 to 889. The cousin of AED, whom he is thought to have murdered to take the throne. He ruled jointly with EOCHA who was King of the Britons of Strathclyde and KENNETH I's grandson. He was defeated and killed in battle at Dundurn by DONALD II.

Giric II (d.1005) King of Scots. Reigned from 997 to

1005. The son of KENNETH III with whom he shared the throne. Both were killed by MALCOLM II in battle at Monzieviard in order to secure his succession to the throne.

Godfred (Crovan) (d.1095) King of the Isle of Man. Reigned from 1079 to 1095. The island kingdom had been held by Orkney rulers since *c*.990 when Godfred landed in 1079. He founded a dynasty of Norse kings which ruled this island until 1265. The legacy of Godfred's kingdom is reflected in the island's present self-governing status.

Grey, Lady Jane (1537-1554) Queen of England and Ireland (only recognized by King's Lynn and Berwick). Reigned for 9 days in 1553. The daughter of Henry Grey, 3rd Marquis of Dorset, and Lady Francis Brandon, the daughter of HENRY VIII's younger sister, Mary. Lady Jane Grey was the 'The Nine Days Queen', the unfortunate victim of a scheme designed by Dudley, the Duke of Northumberland, to give his family the succession. Dudley persuaded the dying heir to the throne, EDWARD VI, to settle the succession on his daughter-in-law and her male heirs in order to stop the throne being taken by either MARY, Queen of Scots or MARY Tudor, both of whom were catholics. When the heir died in 1553 the country would have nothing to do with Northumberland and Edward's sister, Mary Tudor, was proclaimed by the Lord Mayor of London. Lady Jane Grey was never crowned and had only been recognized by King's Lynn and Berwick before being imprisoned in the Tower. She was later beheaded for treason along with her husband.

Gruffydd ap Cynan (b.1055) King of Gwynedd. Reigned from 1081 to 1137. Although born in Ireland, he invaded his ancestral kingdom three times from 1075. He secured it briefly in 1081 before he was captured and imprisoned in Chester. He escaped, reconquered Gwynedd, and resisted two attempts by WILLIAM II to capture him again. He finally rendered homage to HENRY I.

Gruffydd ap Llywelyn (d.1062) King of Gwynedd. Reigned from 1039 to 1063. He briefly ruled all Wales when he annexed Deheubarth in 1055. After several years spent raiding the English border he was captured by a Wessex army at Rhuddlan in 1062 and beheaded. His descendants ruled the kingdom of Powys until 1269.

Guthrum (d.890) King of East Anglia. Reigned from 880 to 890. A Danish army commander who first attacked Wessex in 878. He was defeated by ALFRED at Ethandune and made the Treaty of Wedmore. The treaty required Guthrum and his men to embrace Christianity and accept baptism. With Alfred acting as sponsor, they honoured their oaths and were baptized at the River Aller in Somerset. Guthrum then became King of East Anglia and settled at Cirencester.

H

Halfran (Ragnarson) (d.895) King of York. Reigned from 875 to 883. In 875 he founded the kingdom of York which had thirteen Norse rulers in eighty years.

Hardicanute (1018-1042) King of England and Denmark. Reigned (England) from 1040 to 1042. The only son of CANUTE and Emma of Normandy. The rightful successor to Canute, he was consolidating his dominion over Denmark when his half-brother HAROLD usurped his English throne in 1035. He came to the throne on Harold's death in 1040. Hardicanute's short and unpopular reign is noteworthy for its violence; he had Worcester burned for killing royal tax collectors, he murdered the Earl of Northumbria, and abused the body of his dead brother Harold I by having it flung into a bog. He collapsed at a drunken wedding banquet and died shortly after. He was succeeded by EDWARD the Confessor.

Harold I (Harefoot) (1016-1040) King of England. Reigned from 1035 to 1040. The second son of CANUTE and Elgifu, he succeeded his father CANUTE to the throne of England. Despite being his illegitimate son, he proclaimed himself king and had a rival claimant, Aetheling, son of ETHELRED, blinded and killed. His countrymen, the Danes, maintained him upon the throne while his half-brother was in Denmark. He exiled Emma, mother of HARDICANUTE, and defended his kingdom against vigorous attacks from the Welsh and Scots.

Harold II (1020-1066) King of England. Reigned in 1066. The second son of Godwin, Earl of Kent, and Gytha, sister of CANUTE's Danish brother-in-law. Made powerful by the inheritance of his father's lands in Wessex and Kent, he was a rival to EDWARD THE CONFESSOR for the whole kingdom of England. He successfully defeated Welsh incursions and took control of Hereford before he was shipwrecked in 1064. He was then held by Duke WILLIAM of Normandy and only gained his release by promising to help secure the crown for him. He himself had been named as successor by the dying Edward however, and in early 1066 he stepped into the vacant throne. Claims of a bequest of Edward in favour of the Duke of Normandy led the latter to call upon him to resign the crown. Harold refused and William prepared for invasion. William also instigated Harold's hostile brother, Tostig, to land on the northern coasts of England in conjunction with the King of Norway. The united fleet of these chiefs sailed up the Humber, and landed a numerous body of men, but at Stamford Bridge, in Yorkshire, were totally routed by Harold, whose brother Tostig fell in the battle. Immediately after the battle Harold heard of the landing of the

Duke of Normandy at Pevensey in Sussex, and went there with all the troops he could muster. It was a forced march of over 250 miles completed in nine days, but in the engagement which followed at Senlac, near Hastings, they were narrowly beaten. Harold died on the field, supposedly killed by an arrow, with two of his brothers. With his death there also ended England's 600 years of rule by Anglo-Saxon kings.

Hengest King of Kent. Reigned from 455 to 488. The first of the Jutish kings of Kent, he ruled jointly with his brother HORSA. After being invited by the British king VORTIGERN to help force back the northern Picts, Hengest, along with his brother, turned on the Britons and founded what is referred to in the *Anglo-Saxon Chronicles* as the first Saxon kingdom. His son, AESC, succeeded him.

Henry I (1068-1135) King of England. Reigned from 1100 to 1135. Often surnamed 'Beauclerk' (fine scholar). The youngest son of WILLIAM THE CONQUEROR and Matilda of Flanders. Henry was hunting with WILLIAM RUFUS, when the king was accidentally killed. He immediately rode to London and claimed the throne before he could be challenged by his elder brother Robert Curthose of Normandy, then absent as a Crusader. He soon re-established by charter the laws of EDWARD THE CONFESSOR and did away with the legal abuses William II had let go unchecked. He then introduced measures to stop the seizure of Church lands, and married Matilda, a Saxon daughter of MALCOLM III of Scotland, thus conciliating in turn his people, the Church, and the Scots. Robert landed an army, but was pacified with a pension, and the promise of succession in event of his brother's decease. Soon after, however, Henry invaded Normandy, captured Robert and imprisoned him in Cardiff Castle. The last years of his reign were very troubled. In 1120 his only son William was drowned returning from Normandy, where, three years later, a revolt occurred in favour of Robert's son. The Welsh also were a source of disturbance but he was a capable commander and was never seriously threatened.

In the later years of his reign he was able to strengthen the Norman system of government and administration of justice. He also won from the Church the agreement that the bishops should acknowledge the king as overlord of their extensive secular holdings. Henry appointed as his heir his daughter, MATILDA, whom he had married first to the Emperor Henry V, and then to Geoffrey Plantagenet of Anjou. This laid the basis for a much enlarged kingdom but STEPHEN took the throne from the rightful heir, Matilda, when Henry died of fever in France.

Significant events of Henry I's reign

- 1100 – Charter of Liberties proclaimed.

    Henry marries Edith, daughter of Malcolm III of Scotland.

- 1101 – Robert of Normandy recognises Henry I as king in the Treaty of Alton.

- 1104 – Crusaders capture Acre.
- 1106 – War breaks out with Normandy.
- 1120 – Henry's heir, William, is drowned.
- 1129 – Matilda marries Geoffrey Plantagenet,
  Count de Anjou.

Henry II (1133-1189) King of England. Reigned from 1154 to 1189. The first of the Plantagenet line was born in Normandy, the son of Geoffrey, Count of Anjou, and MATILDA, daughter of HENRY I. Invested with the Duchy of Normandy, by the consent of his mother, in 1150, he succeeded to Anjou and in 1151, and by a marriage with Eleanor of Guienne gained Guienne and Poitou. In 1152 he invaded England to make his claim to the throne, but a compromise was effected, by which STEPHEN was to retain the crown, and Henry to succeed at his death.

He began his reign by destroying the castles, or 'dens of thieves' as he called them, built by rebellious barons in Stephen's time. A man of immense energy, he soon stamped his character on the vast kingdom which stretched from Scotland to the Pyranees. He intended to reform the powers of the Church and began by installing Thomas á Becket as Archbishop of Canterbury. The Constitutions of Clarendon, which placed limitations on the Church's jurisdiction over crimes commited by the clergy, were contested by Becket, however, and he fled the kingdom after quarrelling with the king. They were later reconciled but quarrelled again and Becket was murdered in Canterbury Cathedral by four knights who took Henry's request 'Will someone not rid me of this turbulent priest?' a little too literally. Although sufficiently submissive after Becket's death in the way of penance, Henry only gave up the article in the Constitutions of Clarendon which forbade appeals to the court of Rome in ecclesiastical cases.

Henry began the settlement of Ireland in 1166 after responding to a request by the king of Leinster to resolve a dynastic dispute. His support was commanded by Richard de Clare, Earl of Pembroke, commonly known as Strongbow, who successfully established England's claim to rule Ireland and forced the subservience of all Ireland's regional kings to Henry, who created himself First Lord of Ireland. An earlier papal bull *Laudabiliter*, made by Pope Adrian IV in 1155, had given the approval of the Roman Church for an invasion to bring the Irish Church under its control.

Henry's last years were embittered by his sons, to whom he had assigned various territories. The eldest son, Henry, who had been not only declared heir to England, Normandy, Anjou, Maine, and Touraine, but actually crowned in his father's lifetime, was induced by the French monarch to demand of his father the immediate resignation either of the Kingdom of England or of the dukedom of Normandy. Queen Eleanor excited her other sons, RICHARD and Geoffrey, to make similar claims; WILLIAM of Scotland gave them support. A general invasion of Henry's dominions was begun in 1173 by an attack on the frontiers of Normandy, and an invasion of England by the Scots, attended by considerable disturbance in England. Henry took prompt action; William I of Scotland was captured and forced to acknowledge the English king as overlord. Henry's sons, however, once more became turbulent, and though the deaths of Henry and Geoffrey reduced the number of centres of disturbance, the king was forced to accept humiliating terms from Richard and Philip of France.

Henry II ranks among the greatest English kings both in soldiership and statecraft. He partitioned England into four judiciary districts, and appointed itinerant justices to make regular excursions through them. He revived trial by jury and established it as a right but by the time of his death he was a defeated king, worn out by family revolts.

Significant events of Henry II's reign

- 1155 – Thomas á Beckett appointed Chancellor of England.

  Pope Adrian IV's papal bull gives Henry the right to invade Ireland.

- 1162 – Beckett appointed Archbishop of Canterbury.

- 1164 – The Constitutions of Clarendon issued.

- 1166 – Trial by jury is established at the Assize of Clarendon.

- 1168 – Oxford University founded.

- 1170 – Beckett is murdered.

- 1171 – Henry is acknowledged as Lord of Ireland.

- 1173 – Beckett is canonized.

Henry III (1207-1272) King of England. Reigned
from 1216 to 1272. The eldest son of JOHN by Isabel
of Angouleme, was born at Winchester and succeeded his father at the age of nine. At the time of his
accession the Dauphin of France, Louis, at the head
of a foreign army, supported by a faction of English
nobles, had assumed the reins of government; but
was compelled to quit the country by the Earl of
Pembroke, who was guardian of the young king until
1219. The Treaty of Lambeth followed which established peace between France, the English barons and
supporters of Henry. But as Henry approached to
manhood he displayed a character wholly unfit for
his station. He discarded his most able minister,
Hubert de Burgh, and falsely accused him of treason.
After 1230, when he received homage in Poitou and
Gascony, he began to bestow his chief favours upon
foreigners and installed many of them in government.

His marriage in 1236 with Eleanor of Provence increased the dislike to him felt by his subjects, and although he received frequent grants of money from
Parliament, on condition of confirming the Great
Charter, his conduct after each ratification was as arbitrary as before. At length the nobles rose in rebellion under Simon de Montfort, Earl of Leicester and
husband of the king's sister; and in 1258, at a Parliament held at Oxford, known in history as the Mad
Parliament, obliged the king to sign the body of reso-
lutions known as the Provisions of Oxford. A feud
arose, however, between Montfort and Gloucester,
and Henry recovered some of his power. War again

broke out, and Louis was called in as arbitrator, but his award being favourable to the king, Leicester refused to submit to it. A battle was fought near Lewes, in which Henry was taken prisoner. A convention, called the Mise of Lewes, provided for the future settlement of the kingdom; and in 1265 the first genuine House of Commons was summoned. Leicester, however, was defeated and slain in the battle of Evesham (1265), and Henry was replaced upon the throne.

He was a selfish and petulant king, with few of the personal qualities required to command respect or obedience. In some respects, however, he redeemed himself as patron of the arts. He established the first three colleges of Oxford and initiated the improvements to Westminster Abbey and the construction of Salisbury Cathedral. His son, EDWARD I, succeeded him.

Significant events of Henry III's reign

- 1227 – Henry takes control of the government; Hubert de Burgh remains as adviser.

- 1232 – Hubert de Burgh is dismissed; Peter des Riveaux becomes Treasurer of England.

- 1234 – A revolt led by Richard Marshall is defeated.

- 1258 – The Provisions of Oxford are prompted by a rebellion led by Simon de Montford.

- 1261 – Henry renounces the Provisions.

- 1264 – The Baron's War begins.

- 1265 – The 'Mad' Parliament is called.

    Montford killed at the Battle of Evesham.

Henry IV (1366-1413) King of England and Wales.
Reigned from 1399 to 1413. The eldest son of John
of Gaunt, Duke of Lancaster, fourth son of EDWARD
III, by Blanche of Lancaster, the daughter of Henry,
Duke of Lancaster, great-grandson of HENRY III. In
the reign of RICHARD II he was made Earl of Derby
and Duke of Hereford, but having in 1338 preferred a
charge of treason against Mowbray, Duke of Norfolk, he was banished with his adversary. In the
1390's Henry took part in crusades in Lithuania and
Prussia. On the death of John of Gaunt, Richard
withheld Henry's inheritance, and Henry, landing in
England, deposed the king and had him imprisoned
at Pontefract Castle. The recognition of Henry IV
as king by Parliament was followed by Richard's
death in prison the following year by self-inflicted
starvation.

Henry was king by conquest and election by Parliament, however, and not by heredity. For this reason he had to accept a degree of subservience to his
peers and to conciliate the Church accepted the *De
Heretico Comburendo*, a statute which persecuted
heretics, notably the followers of John Wycliffe,
known as the Lollards. His position was precarious
and there were several plots to depose him which led
to the executions of several noblemen. An insurrection in Wales, however, under Owen Glyndwr proved
more formidable. Glyndwr was a descendant of the
last independent Prince of Wales and sought full independence for his principality. He launched a gue-
rilla campaign against the English in 1401 and made

a Treaty with France who sent an army to help him. For the next ten years all attempts to subdue him failed.

Henry was also troubled by the Scots and the Percy family of Northumberland. In 1402 the Scots were decisively defeated by the Percies at Homildon Hill and their leader, the Earl of Douglas, was captured. An order from Henry not to permit the ransom of Douglas and other Scottish prisoners was regarded as an indignity by the Percies, who let Douglas free, made an alliance with him, and joined Glyndwr. The king met the insurgents at Shrewsbury and the battle ended in defeat for the Percies. The Earl of Northumberland was pardoned, but a few of the insurgents were executed. A new insurrection, headed by the Earl of Nottingham and Scrope, Archbishop of York, broke out in 1405, but was suppressed. The same year, JAMES, the son and heir to King ROBERT III of Scotland, was captured at sea on his way to France, and imprisoned in England. The rest of Henry's reign was comparatively untroubled and he eventually died after contracting a leprosy-like illness. He was succeeded by his son, HENRY V.

Significant events of Henry IV's reign

- 1400 – Richard II dies in prison.

    Geoffrey Chaucer dies.

- 1401 – Statute of *De Heretico Comburendo* leads
    to many being burned at the stake.

- 1403 – The Percy family rebellion is defeated at
    Shewesbury.

- 1404 – Glyndwr sets up Welsh Parliament.
- 1405 – French troops land in Wales.
- 1411 – Construction of the Guildhall in London begins.

Henry V (1387-1422) King of England. Reigned from 1413 to 1422. The only surviving son of HENRY IV and Mary de Bohun. He showed a wisdom in kingship in marked contrast to a somewhat reckless youth. As Prince of Wales he had fought against Welsh rebels and prided himself in his abilities as a soldier. On becoming king he acted quickly to thwart an attempt by a group of nobles to place his cousin, Edmund Mortimer, Earl of March, on the throne. He also carried on the persecution of the Lollards and sent many to their deaths. Like his father, his claim to the throne was doubtful, and he busied himself with foreign affairs in order to divert attention from domestic difficulties.

The struggle in France between the factions of the Dukes of Orleans and Burgundy afforded Henry a tempting opportunity for reviving the claims of his predecessors to the French crown. He accordingly landed near Harfleur in 1415, and though its capture cost him more than half his army, he decided to return to England by way of Calais. A large French army endeavoured to intercept him at the plain of Agincourt, but was completely routed. It is thought that as many as 6,000 Frenchmen died while less than 400 English lost their lives. A year later the French were defeated at sea by the Duke of Bedford.

In 1417 the liberal grants of the Commons enabled Henry once more to invade Normandy with 25,000 men. The assassination of the Duke of Burgundy, which induced his son and successor to join Henry, greatly added to his power and the alliance was soon followed by the famous Treaty of Troyes, by which Henry engaged to marry the Princess Catherine and to leave Charles VI in possession of the crown, on condition that it should go to Henry and his heirs at his death. He returned in triumph to England, but on the defeat of his brother, the Duke of Clarence, in Normandy by the Earl of Buchan, he again set out for France, drove back the army of the dauphin, and entered Paris. All his great projects seemed about to be realized when he died of fever at Vincennes, at the age of thirty-five having reigned for ten years.

An adventurous, headstrong leader, Henry pursued his policies with great zeal and proved himself to be a shrewd military tactician as well as an able politician. His campaign in France had the effect of uniting his nobles in a common cause, thus diverting attention from domestic plots to unthrone him. His ten-month-old son, HENRY VI, succeeded him as king of both England and France.

Significant events of Henry V's reign

- 1415 – The Cambridge plot is thwarted.

    Battle of Agincourt.

- 1416 – Welsh leader Glyndwr dies.

- 1420 – The Treaty of Troyes makes Henry heir to the French throne

Henry VI (1421-1471) King of England and Wales. Reigned from 1422 to 1461 and from 1470 to 1471. The only son of HENRY V and Catherine of Valois, he succeeded to the throne on the death of his father when he was less than one year old. In his minority, the government of the kingdom was placed in the hands of his uncle Humphrey, Duke of Gloucester, who was made Protector of the Realm of England. A few weeks after Henry's succession Charles VI of France died, when, in accordance with the Treaty of Troyes, Henry was proclaimed King of France. His uncle John, Duke of Bedford was appointed Regent of France. The war which followed at first proved favourable to the English, but by the heroism of Joan of Arc, who claimed to have been inspired by a vision telling her to drive the English from France, the confidence of the French people was restored. Joan of Arc was captured and burnt at the stake in Rouen but Henry eventually lost all his possessions in France with the exception of Calais.

When Henry assumed personal rule at the age of fifteen the government of England was being conducted by rival ministers of the Houses of York and Lancaster. The fact that he also suffered from bouts of mental illness gave these houses greater power and their rivalry increased. In 1453 his wife, Margaret of Anjou, bore him a son but within the year his mind had failed him to such a degree that he had to submit to the rule of a Protector, Richard, Duke of York. Fighting soon broke out between the Houses of York and Lancaster, the rival factions in government, and the appointment of York was annulled the following year, the king having recovered his faculties. York retired to the north, and being joined by his adherents, marched upon London. He encountered and defeated the king's Lancastrian army at St Albans, the first battle of the thirty years' War of the Roses. The king again becoming deranged, York was once more made Protector. Four years of peace followed, but the struggle was soon renewed. A Yorkist army led by Richard Neville, Earl of Warwick, defeated the Lancastrian forces at Bloreheath, but they recovered to win over the Yorkists at Ludford. The Lancastrians then declared York a traitor at a session of Parliament held in Coventry. Neville's army in return defeated the Lancastrians at Northampton and captured Henry. Following this victory York was restored as Protector and Henry's wife, Margaret, fled to Scotland. She returned with an army which defeated the Yorkists at Wakefield and killed their leader, Richard of York, who was replaced by his son, EDWARD, as Duke of York. His army then defeated the Lancastrians at Mortimer's Cross and Warwick engaged Margaret's forces at the second Battle of St Albans. Warwick was unsuccessful at first but finally defeated Margaret's army at the Battle of Towton and declared Edward, Duke of York, as king.

Further revolts by the Lanacastrians were suppressed and Henry was captured and imprisoned in the Tower of London following Warwick's victory at the Battle of Hexham. Edward owed his crown to

Warrick however, and it was inevitable that the next stage of the struggle would be between the king-maker and the king. After gaining the upper hand at Edgecote, Warrick was at lenghth banished by the king only to return, allied with Margaret, to attempt a restoration of Henry. This they acheived in 1470, but it was to be a brief affair; Edward soon returned and defeated Warrick at the Battle of Barnet and Margaret at the Battle of Tewkesbury. Warrick and Margaret's son, Edward, were both killed in the fighting and shortly after Henry was murdered in the Tower. The Wars of the Roses did not end until 1485 when the Lancastrian heir and claimant to the throne, HENRY Tudor, defeated RICHARD III, the brother of EDWARD IV.

Henry VI had been a pious and well-intentioned but hopelessly incompetent ruler. Throughout his life he had been deeply religious and had a passion for education and building. His principal claim to re-membrance is that he founded Eton College and King's College, Cambridge.

Significant events of Henry VI's reign

- 1422 – Henry becomes king of France on the death of Charles VI.
- 1429 – Joan of Arc begins the rout of the English.
- 1431 – Joan of Arc is burned at the stake.
- 1437 – Henry VI assumes control of government.
- 1453 – The English are expelled from France, ending of the Hundred Years' War.

- 1454 – Richard, Duke of York, becomes
  Protector.

- 1455 – The Wars of the Roses begin when
  Richard is dismissed as Protector and
  rebels against King Henry.

- 1461 – Richard's son Edward deposes Henry.

- 1470 – Henry briefly regains the crown.

Henry VII (1457-1509) King of England. Reigned
from 1485 to 1509. The first of the Tudor kings,
Henry was the son of Edmund, Earl of Richmond,
son of Owen Tudor and Catherine of France, widow
of HENRY V. His mother, Margaret, was the only child
of John, Duke of Somerset, grandson of John of
Gaunt. After the battle of Tewkesbury he was carried
by his uncle, the Earl of Pembroke, to Brittany, and
on the usurpation of RICHARD III was naturally turned
to as the representative of the House of Lancaster. In
1485 he assembled a small body of troops in Brittany, and, having landed at Milford Haven, defeated
Richard III at Bosworth. Henry was proclaimed king
on the field of battle, his right being subsequently
recognized by Parliament. In 1486 he married Elizabeth, daughter of EDWARD IV and heiress of the
House of York, and thus united the claims of the rival
Houses of York and Lancaster.

His reign was troubled by repeated insurrections,
of which the chief were that headed by Lord Lovel
and the Staffords (1486), and the impostures of Lambert Simnel (1487) and Perkin Warbeck (1496–99).
In order to strengthen England's prestige he made

important marriage alliances. He brought about a match between the Infanta Catherine, daughter of Ferdinand of Aragon and Isabella of Castile, and his eldest son Arthur. On the death of Arthur, in order to retain the dowry of this princess, he caused his remaining son HENRY to marry the widow by Papal dispensation, an event which, in the sequel, led to a separation from Rome. He married his eldest daughter to JAMES IV, King of Scots, from which marriage there ultimately resulted the union of the two crowns.

The problem of the English barons was still present however, and he set about breaking their power by reviving the Court of Star Chamber. This prevented the barons from raising private armies and allowed them to be tried if they broke the law. He also did much to strengthen England's commercial activities and took an interest in the development of trading in North America. His fiscal policies were often criticised as being largely for the benefit of the royal exchequer and in his latter years this avarice became increasingly marked. Two exchequer judges, Empson and Dudley, were being employed in all sorts of extortion and chicanery in order to gratify the royal purse. His reign, however, was in the main beneficent. Its freedom from wars permitted the development of the internal resources of the country. His policy of depressing the feudal nobility, which proportionably exalted the middle ranks, was highly salutary. For a time, however, the power lost by the aristocracy gave an undue preponderance to that of the crown.

A cultured man, Henry also brought European

scholars to England, patronized the printer William Claxton, and initiated what came to be called the 'Revival of Learning'. In his later years he suffered from arthritis and gout and died at the age of 52. His eight children by Elizabeth of York included his successor, HENRY VIII.

Significant events of Henry VII's reign

- 1485 – Henry defeats Richard III at Bosworth and is declared King of England.

  The Yeoman of the Guard is formed.

- 1486 – The Houses of York and Lancaster are joined with the marriage of Henry to Elizabeth of York.

- 1487 – A rebellion on behalf of the pretender Lambert Simnel is thwarted.

- 1492 – Henry defeats another attempt to dethrone him led by Perkin Warbeck.

  America discovered by Columbus.

- 1497 – John Cabot discovers Newfoundland.

- 1502 – Henry's daughter is married to James IV of Scotland.

Henry VIII (1491-1547) King of England and Ireland (from 1542). Reigned from 1509 to 1547. The second son of HENRY VII and Elizabeth of York, he succeeded his father as king at the age of eighteen. Although well-educated and opinionated, the young king at first had no enthusiasm for politics or personal rule. He chose instead to leave the business of government to the very capable Cardinal Wolsey. He administered with great skill and increased England's trade and standing abroad.

Henry stained the finances of his kingdom however, through a series of costly wars. The success of the English at the Battle of the Spurs (1513) was succeeded by no adequate result, the taking of Tournay being the only fruit of this expensive expedition. In the meantime, success attended the English arms at home with JAMES IV of Scotland being completely defeated and slain at Flodden Field in 1513. Henry, however, granted peace to the Queen of Scotland, his sister, and established an influence which rendered his kingdom long secure on that side. He soon after made peace with France, retaining Tournay and receiving a large sum of money. After the election of Charles V to the German Empire, both Charles and the French king, Francis I, sought the alliance of England. A friendly meeting took place between Henry and Francis at the Field of the Cloth of Gold (1520), but the interest of Charles preponderated, and Henry soon after again declared war against France.

In 1529 came the determination of the king to divorce his wife Catherine, who was older than he, had borne him no male heir, and had, moreover, been in the first place the wife of his elder brother. The last of these points was the alleged ground for seeking divorce, though Henry was probably influenced largely by his attachment to Anne Boleyn, one of the queen's maids of honour. Wolsey, for his own ends, had at first been active in promoting the divorce, but drew back and procrastinated when it became apparent that Anne Boleyn would be Catherine's successor. This delay cost Wolsey his power and the papacy its authority in England. Wolset was accused of treason but died before he could be brought to trail. Henry eagerly caught at the advice of Thomas Cranmer, afterwards Archbishop of Canterbury, to refer the case to the Universities, from which he soon got the decision that he desired. In 1533 his marriage with Catherine was declared null and an anticipatory private marriage with Anne Boleyn declared lawful; and as these decisions were not recognized by the Pope, two Acts of Parliament were obtained, one in 1534 setting aside the authority of the chief pontiff in England, the other in 1335 declaring Henry the supreme head of the Church. But although Henry discarded the authority of the Roman Church, he adhered to its theological tenets, and while, on the one hand, he executed Bishop Fisher and Sir Thomas More for refusing the oath of supremacy, he brought many of the reformers to the stake. Finding that the monks and friars in England were the most direct advocates of the Papal authority, and a constant source of disaffection, he suppressed the monasteries by Act of Parliament, and thereby inflicted an incurable wound upon the Catholic religion in England. The fall of Anne Boleyn, was, however, unfavourable for a time to the reformers.

Henry then married Jane Seymour, and the birth of a son in 1537 fulfilled his wish for a male heir. The death of the queen was followed in 1540 by Henry's marriage with Anne of Cleves, the negotiations of which were conducted by Cromwell. The king's dislike to his wife, which resulted in another divorce became extended to the minister who had proposed the union, and Cromwell's disgrace and death soon followed. A marriage with Catherine Howard in 1541 proved no happier, and in 1542 she was executed on a charge of infidelity. In 1543 he married his sixth wife, Catherine Parr, a lady secretly inclined to the Reformation, who survived the king.

In the meantime Scotland and France had renewed their alliance, and England became again involved in war. JAMES V ravaged the borders, but was defeated at Solway Moss in 1542, and in 1544 Boulogne was captured, Henry having again allied himself with Charles V. Charles, however, soon withdrew, and Henry maintained the war alone until 1546. War and his sense of isolation now so much aggravated the natural violence of Henry that his oldest friends fell victims to his tyranny. The Duke of Norfolk was committed to the Tower, and his son the Earl of Surrey, was executed.

During his reign it is estimated that Henry had at least seventy thousand people executed for various offences. As well as the brutality shown to his subjects, he also frequently proved himself to be disloyal to his wives and advisors. His driving ambition, however, was to secure a male heir for the throne and he cared little about his public image so long as this goal was acheived. His only son by Jane Seymour, EDWARD VI, succeeded him.

Significant events of Henry VIII's reign

- 1509 – Henry marries Catherine of Aragon.

- 1513 – James IV of Scotland is killed at the
        Battle of Flodden.

- 1515- Thomas Wolsey is made Chancellor of
        England.

- 1517 – Martin Luther protests against the
        indulgences of the Roman Catholic
        church at Wittenburg.

- 1520 – Francois I of France meets Henry at the
        Field of the Cloth of Gold.

- 1529 – Cardinal Wolsey is accused of treason.

        Sir Thomas More becomes Chancellor of
        England.

- 1532 – Sir Thomas More resigns.

- 1533 – Archbishop Thomas Cranmer annulls
        Henry and Catherine's marriage.

        Henry marries Anne Boleyn.

        The Pope excommunicates Henry.

- 1534 – Act of Supremacy makes Henry the head
        of the Church in England.

- 1535 – Sir Thomas More does not accept the Act
        of Supremacy and is put to death.

- 1536 – Anne Boleyn is executed; Henry marries
        Jane Seymour.

        The Act of Union unites England and
        Wales.

        The dissolution of the monasteries
        begins.

- 1537 – Jane Seymour gives dies.
- 1540 – Henry marries Anne of Cleves and divorces her six months later.

  Henry marries Catherine Howard.
- 1542 – Catherine Howard charged with treason and put to death.
- 1543 – Henry marries Catherine Parr.

Hlothere (d.685) King of Kent. Reigned from 673 to 685. The younger brother of EGBERT I, he was sole ruler, and then from 676, joint ruler with SUAEBHARD of Essex. Early in his reign he faced an invasion from Mercia and died in battle during a later South Saxon conquest.

Horsa (d.455) King of Kent. Reigned in 455. With his brother HENGEST he became joint ruler after being invited by VORTIGERN to help fight off raids from the north. The first Jutish kings soon established themselves despite Horsa's early death in battle at Aegelsthrep (Aylesford, near Maidstone)

Hywel ab Idwal (the Bad) King of Gwynedd. Reigned from 979 to 985. A descendant of RHODI MWAR, he deposed his father IAGO AP IDWAL.

Hywel Dda (the Good) (d.950) King of Gwynedd. Reigned from 904 to 950. A grandson of RHODI MWAR, he briefly united north and south Wales under his governorship. By marriage to princess Elen, daughter of the king of Dyfed, he secured that kingdom (c.904) and soon extended his realm into the area of south Wales known as Deheubarth. He also absorbed Powys but had to acknowledge EDWARD the Elder and later ETHELSATAN as overlords in light of threatened invasions by the Danes. The law code which he is credited with initiating (the Laws of Hywel) still survives in a 13th century manuscript and he was the only Welsh ruler to issue a coinage. He went on a pilgrimage to Rome in 928.

I

Iago I ab Idwal (d.c.980) King of Gwynedd. He reigned from 950 to 979. Deposed by his son, HYWEL AB IDWAL.

Iago II ab Idwal (d.c.1040) King of Gwynedd. He reigned from 1023 to 1039. The granson of the first IAGO and father of GRUFFYDD AP CYAN.

Ida (d.c.568) King of Bernicia. Reigned from 547 to 568. According to the *Anglo-Saxon Chronicle* he captured the Bernician stronghold of Banburgh and, with his son AELLE as king of Deira, effectivley ruled most of Northumbria. This name for this kingdom comes from *Northanhymbre*, the Old English for 'people north of the River Humber'.

Idwal Foel (Idwal the Bald) King of Gwynedd. Reigned from 916 to 942. The son of ANARAWD, he was killed rebelling against EDMUND II of England. HYWEL DDA succeeded him.

Indulf King of Scots. Reigned from 954 to 962. Succeeded his uncle MALCOLM I to the throne and abdicated eight years later in favour of DUFF, Malcolm's son. He died at St Andrews and was buried at Iona

Ine (d.c.728) King of Wessex. Reigned from 688 to 726. One of the most powerful Wessex rulers, he defeated the South Saxons in battle in 722 and 725 and the Cornish Britons in 710. He set up a port at Southampton and founded the monastery at Glastonbury (his sister, Cuthburh, founded a monastery at Wimborne in Dorset). His greatest achievement, however, was the important law code he compiled between 690 and 693 which reveals a growing sophistication in the consideration of the concepts of kingship and royal authority. He abdicated and retired to Rome.

J

James I (1394-1437) King of Scots. Reigned from 1406 to 1437. The son of ROBERT III by Annabella Drummond. Following the death of James's brother, Robert wished him to be conveyed to France in order to escape the intrigues of his uncle the first Duke of Albany. The ship in which he was being conveyed was captured by an English squadron off Flamborough Head, and the prince was taken prisoner to London were he received an education from HENRY IV. To relieve the tedium of captivity, he applied himself to those poetical and literary pursuits in which he so highly distinguished himself. Robert III died in 1406, but James was not allowed to return to his kingdom until a ransom had been paid and hostages handed over to act as security. After the Treaty of London he was freed and crowned at Scone. Before his departure he married Joanna Beaufort, daughter of the Earl of Somerset. On his return to Scotland he had the second Duke of Albany and his son Murdoch executed as traitors, and proceeded to carry on vigorous reforms, and, above all, to improve his revenue and curb the ambition and lawlessness of the nobles. The nobility, headed by the Earl of Atholl,

exasperated by the decline of their power, formed a
plot against his life, and assassinated him at Perth in
1437, where he was buried. His poem *The King's
Quiar* (or King's Book) entitles him to high rank
among the followers of Chaucer. He was succeeded
by his son JAMES II.

Significant events of James I's reign

- 1406 – James is captured by the English en route
  to France and is held in the Tower.
- 1423 – Treaty of London agreed.
- 1424 – James is freed on a ransom.

James I of England. *See* **James VI** of Scots.

James II (1430-1460) King of Scots. Reigned from
1437 to 1460. The surviving twin son of JAMES I and
Queen Joan, he was only seven years old when his
father was assassinated. He was the first king to be
crowned at Kelso Abbey rather than Scone. During
the minority his kingdom was distracted by struggles
for power between his tutors Livingston and
Crichton and the great House of Douglas. Crichton
had the Earl Douglas murdered at what would come
to be known as the 'Black Dinner' at Edinburgh castle with the young king in attendance. After assuming
his full powers as king, James still found his position
menaced by the great family of Douglas, and he invited the 8th Earl of Douglas to Stirling Castle, to
persuade him to abandon a league of nobles which
had been formed in opposition to the Crown. The interview ended in the king stabbing his guest and his

bodyguard killing him. The civil war which followed was won by James and three years later Parliament announced the forfeiture of the Douglas territories.

Having finally brought the nobles under control, James, who due to a birthmark was nicknamed 'Fiery Face', consolidated his kingdom to the point where even the Lords of the Isles were involved in his attempt to take back Roxburgh from the English. He was killed by the bursting of a cannon at this siege. By his wife, Mary of Gueldres, he had four sons and was succeeded by his eldest, JAMES III.

Significant events of James II's reign

- 1450 – Glasgow University is founded.
- 1455 – James II defeats the 'Black' Douglas family.

James II of Great Britain and Ireland. (1633-1701). Reigned from 1685 to 1688. The second son of CHARLES I and Henrietta Maria of France, he was immediately created Duke of York. During the Civil War he escaped from England and served with distinction in the French army under Turenne, and in the Spanish army under Condé. At the Restoration in 1660 he got the command of the fleet as Lord High-Admiral. He had previously married Anne, daughter of Chancellor Hyde, afterward Lord Clarendon. In 1671 she died, leaving two daughters, Mary and Anne, both of whom were subsequently sovereigns of England and Scotland. Having openly avowed the Roman Catholic faith, on the Test Act being passed to prevent Roman Catholics from holding public employments he was obliged to resign his command. He was afterwards sent to Scotland as Lord High Commissioner, where he persecuted the Covenanters.

He succeeded his brother as king in 1685, and at once set himself to attain absolute power. His conversion to Catholicism had made him unpopular however, and a rebellion was initiated by the Duke of Monmouth (his nephew). This was easily put down (the Battle of Sedgmoor in 1685 was the last to be fought on English soil) and encouraged the king in his arbitrary measures. After a series of trials, known as the Bloody Assizes, 320 rebels were executed and 800 transported as slaves.

He then accepted a pension from Louis XIV that he might more readily effect his purposes, especially that of restoring the Roman Catholic religion. The Declaration of Indulgence followed which led to the imprisonment of seven bishops who opposed the suspension of penal laws against Roman Catholics. The bishops were later found not guilty of the charge laid at them, that of sedition, and were freed. Things came to a head in the Revolution of 1688 which immediately followed the birth of a male heir by the king's second wife, Mary of Modena (the future 'Old Pretender', recognized by Jacobites as James III of England and James VIII of Scotland). Fearing a Catholic tyranny the king's opponents invited his son-in-law, WILLIAM of Orange, to claim the throne. He landed in November 1688; James found himself completely deserted and fled to France, where he was received with great kindness and hospitality by Louis

XIV. Parliament declared James to have abdicated soon after and William accepted the throne. James attempted the recovery of Ireland; but the battle of the Boyne, fought in 1690, compelled him to return to France. All succeeding projects for his restoration proved equally abortive, and he spent the last years of his life in ascetic devotion. He died of a stroke at St Germain in 1701.

Significant events of James II's reign

- 1685 – Monmouth fails to depose the king. The Bloody Assizes follow.

- 1686 – James disregards the Test Act and Catholics are appointed to public office.

- 1688 – William III lands in England and James flees to France.

  James is deemed by Parliament to have abdicated.

James III (1451-1488) King of Scots. The son of JAMES II and Mary of Guelders. Succeeding his father at the age of nine, the kingdom during his minority was governed in turn by Bishop Kennedy and the Boyd family. James throughout his reign was much under the influence of favourites, and he quarrelled with his brothers; one, the Earl of Mar, was reputedly murdered and another, the Duke of Albany, forced to flee to France. Albany obtained English aid and later invaded Scotland with hopes of being crowned as Alexander IV. When James marched to meet him, the nobles seized and hanged some of his favourites, including Cochrane, an architect, who was specially unpopular. Albany was proclaimed 'Lieutenant General of the Realm' but was soon afterwards expelled.

James continued to be on bad terms with his nobles, and was eventually defeated by a rebellion led by his son, later James IV, in 1469. After a military defeat at Sauchiburn, near Stirling, the king was murdered, allegedly by a soldier disguised as a priest. By his marriage with Margaret, daughter of Christian I of Denmark and Norway, he brought Orkney and Shetland into the Kingdom of Scotland. They had three sons.

Significant events of James III's reign

- 1470 – Work begins on the Great Hall at Stirling Castle.
- 1472 – Scotland gains Orkney and Shetland isles from Norway as a royal wedding dowry.
- 1482 – Scotland loses Berwick to the English.
- 1488 – James IV leads the rebel noblemen at the Battle of Sauchieburn.

James IV (1473-1513) King of Scots. Reigned from 1488 to 1513. The son of JAMES III, he was in his sixteenth year when he succeeded to the throne, and was, either voluntarily or by compulsion, on the side of the nobles who rebelled against his father. He was not judged to require a regent, and, feeling great remorse for the manner in which he became king, carried out his duties admirably. During his reign the ancient enmity between the king and the nobility seems to have ceased. His frankness and bravery won him the people's love, and he ruled with vigour, administered justice with impartiality, and passed important laws. HENRY VII, then king of England, tried to obtain a union with Scotland by politic measures, and in 1503 James married his daughter, Margaret. This was later to become the basis for Stuart rule in England. A period of peace and prosperity followed. French influence, however, and the discourtesy of HENRY VIII in retaining the jewels of his sister and in encouraging the border chieftains hostile to Scotland, led to angry negotiations which ended in war.

Siding with France in 1513, James invaded England with a large force and, despite papal excommunication and his adviser's pleas for caution, engaged in battle. Together with many of his nobles he perished at Flodden Field having fought at the heart of the battle. He was the last British king to die in battle and it was later said of him that he was 'more courageous than a king should be'

He is credited with sponsoring Renaissance values in Scotland and did much to broaden education in his kingdom. But by leaving an heir to the throne, JAMES V, who was barely more than one year-old he had put Scotland's independence in jeopardy.

Significant events of James IV's reign

- 1493 – James subdues the last Lord of the Isles and assumes the title himself.
- 1495 – Aberdeen University founded.
- 1496 – The Scottish Parliament passes education legislation.

- 1503 – James marries the daughter of Henry VII, Margaret Tudor.

- 1507 – Scotland's first printing press is set up in Edinburgh by Andrew Myllar.

- 1513 – James invades England.

James V (1512-1542) King of Scots. Reigned from 1513 to 1542. Succeeded his father, JAMES IV, who had fallen at Flodden, when he was only eighteen months old. His cousin, the Duke of Albany, a Frenchman by birth and education, was the regent during his childhood. Owing to Albany's incompetence and the intrigues of the queen mother, Margaret of England, the period of his long minority was one of lawlessness and gross misgovernment. James assumed the reins of government in his seventeenth year. James V was culturally literate (he renovated several palaces including Linlithgow) but was morally wanting; having at least six illegitimate children and reputedly keeping low company. In order to increase his wealth he married Magdalen, daughter of Francis I of France, in 1537 but she died just seven months later. On her death James married Mary of Lorraine, daughter of the Duke of Guise, and obtained a large dowry.

James was able to exploit the fears of the Pope that Scotland would follow England in making the king head of the church; in return for his commitment to Rome, James received the right to appoint bishops and benefitted from payments from the Church. HENRY VIII, having broken with Rome, and eager to gain his nephew over to his views, proposed an interview at York, but James never came, and it is known that Henry hoped to kidnap him. A rupture took place between the two kingdoms and war was declared. James was ill supported by his nobles, and after some initial success in holding off an English invasion, his army was crushed at Solway Moss. The defeat destroyed him and he died a broken king only seven days after the birth of his daughter, MARY, who became Queen of Scots.

Significant events of James V's reign

- 1532 – The Court of Session, central court of civil justice, is established.

- 1537 – James marries Madeleine de Valois, but she dies shortly after.

- 1538 – James marries Mary of Guise.

- 1542 – Mary of Guise gives birth to Mary, later Mary Queen of Scots.

- 1542 – The Scots invade England and are routed at the Battle of Solway Moss.

James VI of Scots and **I of England** (1566-1625). Reigned (as James VI) from 1567 to 1625 and (as James I) from 1603 to 1625. The only son of MARY, Queen of Scots, and Henry Stuart, Lord Darnley. When James succeeded ELIZABETH I as King of England he had already been on the throne in Scotland for 36 years. He was first crowned at Stirling aged 13 months and at his coronation endured a lengthy sermon from John Knox. His childhood was passed under the direction of the Earl of Mar, and the tuition of the famous Buchanan. He had much trouble with his nobles, a party of whom made him captive at Ruthven Castle in 1582; but a counter party soon set him free. These disputes were connected with the ecclesiastical controversies of this period, James, from his youth onwards, being determined to destroy the power of the Presbyterian clergy. When his mother's life was in danger, he did not exert himself to any great extent on her behalf and when her execution took place he did not venture upon war. In 1589 he married Princess Anne of Denmark. James took an active interest in the North Berwick witch trials of 1591 in which several witches were accused of provoking a storm in the Firth of Forth, as the king was returning from Denmark with his bride. It was probably the Earl of Bothwell, an enemy of the king, who was these behind events. He was imprisoned but later escaped. He had little time for the nobility of Scotland, preferring instead to be a king of the commoners. He was also a firm believer in the Divine Right of Kings, the doctrine in which kings are appointed by God and were therefore unanswerable to other men.

In 1603 James succeeded to the crown of England, on the death of Elizabeth, and proceeded to London bringing with him his favourites from the Scottish court which somewhat alienated the English courtiers. One of the early events of his reign was the Gunpowder Plot in which a group of fanatical Catholics hoped to blow up the king and all his ministers.

He soon allowed his lofty notions of divine right to become known, got into trouble with Parliament, and afterwards endeavoured to rule as an absolute monarch, levying taxes and demanding loans in an arbitrary manner. In matters of religion he succeeded in establishing Episcopacy in Scotland and forced English Puritans to conform to the Anglican Church. He also began the plantation of Scottish and English settlers in Ireland (1611) and curbed the powers of Catholic nobles who objected to their country being treated like a colony.

James was man of peace however, and sought at all costs to keep his people out of war. This led to a decline of the navy and a loss of influence overseas as the government did little to support the new colonies. In 1621 the Thirty Years War of Religion, which involved almost all of Europe, began and one of the Protestant leaders was the German prince who had married James's daughter. Elizabeth (this alliance also ultimately brought the present royal family to the throne). He wished to marry his son, Charles, Prince of Wales, to a Spanish princess, but this was blocked by Paliament, and war was declared against Spain.

James, though possessed of some good abilities had many defects as a ruler, prominent among them being subservience to unworthy favourites. He was also vain, pedantic, and gross in his tastes and habits. He was well-educated and enjoyed being called 'the British Solomon'; Henry IV of France is thought to have coined his more enduring nickname, 'the wisest fool in Christendom'. In his reign the authorized translation of the Bible was executed. He died at Hertfordshire of kidney failure leaving seven children including his successor, CHARLES I.

Significant events of James's reign

- 1591 – The North Berwick witchtrials.
- 1603 – James VI of Scotland ascends the English throne to become James I of England.
- 1605 – The Gunpowder Plot is thwarted.

  Shakespeare writes *King Lear*.
- 1607 – The English Parliament rejects proposals to unite Scotland and England.

  The English colony of Virginia is founded.
- 1611 – The publication of the Authorized Version of the Bible.
- 1614 – James dissolves the 'Addled Parliament' which has failed to pass any legislation.
- 1616 – Shakespeare dies.
- 1618 – Accused of treason, Sir Walter Releigh is put to death.
- 1620 – The Pilgrim Fathers reach Cape Cod in the *Mayflower* and found New Plymouth.

John (1167-1216) King of England. Reigned from 1199 to 1216. The youngest son of HENRY II, by Eleanor of Guienne. Being left without any particular provision, he got the name of 'Sans Terre' or 'Lackland'; but his brother, RICHARD I, on his accession conferred large possessions on him. He obtained the crown on the death of Richard in 1199 although the French provinces of Anjou, Touraine, and Maine declared for his nephew, Arthur of Brittany, who was linearly the rightful heir, then with the king of France. A war ensued, in which John recovered the revolted provinces and received homage from Arthur. In 1201 some disturbances again broke out in France, and the young Arthur, who had joined the malcontents, was captured and confined in the castle of Falaise, and afterwards in that of Rouen, where he died. John was universally suspected of his nephew's death, and the states of Brittany summoned him before his liege lord Philip to answer the charge of murder, and in the war which followed John lost Normandy, Anjou, Maine, and Touraine.

In 1205 his great quarrel with the Pope began regarding the election to the see of Canterbury, to which the Pope had nominated Stephen Langton. The result was that Innocent III laid the whole kingdom under an interdict, and in 1211 issued a Bull deposing John. Philip of France was commissioned to execute the decree, and was already preparing an expedition when John made abject submission to the Pope, even agreeing to hold his kingdom as a vassal of the Pope (1213). John's arbitrary proceedings led to the rising of his nobles, and he was compelled to sign the Magna Carta or Great Charter, in 1215. This charter set out to curtail abuses of royal power in matters of taxation, religion, justice and foreign policy. But John did not mean to keep the agreement, and obtaining a Bull from the Pope annulling the charter, he raised an army of mercenaries and commenced war. The barons, in despair, offered the crown of England to Prince Louis of France, who accordingly landed at Sandwich in 1216, and, after capturing the Tower of London, was received as lawful sovereign. The issue was still doubtful when John was taken ill and died of dysentery at Newark later that year.

Significant events of John's reign

- 1202 – Wars with the French king, Philip II, commence.
- 1206 – Pope Innocent III nominates Stephen Langton as Archbishop of Canterbury.
- 1208 – The Pope's interdict prohibits almost all church services in England.
- 1209 – John is excommunicated.
- 1212 – Pope proclaims that John is not the rightful King of England.
- 1213 – John gives way to the Pope's demands.
- 1214 – Franch defeat the English at Bouvines.

   English barons meet at Bury St Edmunds.
- 1215 – John reluctantly signs the Magna Carta.

   Civil war breaks out when the Pope declares that John need not heed the terms of the Magns Carta .
- 1216 – The French join the fray at the invitation of the barons.

K

Kenneth (I) mac-Alpin (d.858) King of Scots. Reigned from 841 (Scots) and *c*.844 (Picts) to 858. The son of ALPIN, the 34th King of Dalriadan Scots. He united the kingdoms of Scots and Picts by exploiting a period of Pictish weakness due in part to devastating Scandinavian attacks on Pictland although he also had a claim to the pictish kingship by maternal descent. An ambitious and warlike ruler, Kenneth had completely conquered the Picts by 846. In order to eliminate any opposition to his rule it is thought that he asked the heads of important Pict families to dine with him around this time and had them killed when they fell into a concealed pit he had had dug behind the benches on which they were invited to sit.

He moved the centre of his kingdom as part of the general Dalriadic migration into the lands of the Picts, possibly installing the new centre at Forteviot, the old Pictish centre. In 849 he moved the relics of St Columba to Dunkeld and either founded or enlarged a religious centre there. Kenneth's reign was not a peaceful one and he made frequent raids on Lothian and on the Saxons and was raided by Britons, Danes and Vikings.

Kenneth established Scone as a royal and holy centre and made it the place for the inauguration of kings of Alba, as the kingdom was then known. Although it cannot be said with any certainty it has been suggested that it was he who brought the symbolic Stone of Destiny to Scone. On his death through illness he was suceeded by his brother, DONALD I.

Kenneth II (d.995) King of Scots. Reigned from 971 to 995. The son of DUFF, he succeeded CUILEAN in 971. During his reign he was able to secure Lothian as part of his kingdom by recognizing EDGAR, king of England, as his overlord. He was murdered in 995 under mysterious circumstances following a dispute regarding the succession. He was succeeded by CONSTANTINE III, but his son later took the throne as MALCOLM II.

Kenneth III (d.1005) King of Scots. Reigned from 997 to 1005. He ruled jointly with his son, GIRIC II, and both were killed in battle at Monzieviard by MALCOLM II who then ascended the throne.

Kineth (d.843) King of the Picts. Reigned from 842 to 843. The son of UURAD, he is thought to have killed his brother BRED to take the throne. He in turn was usurped and murdered by BRUDE, his nephew.

L

Llywelyn ap Gruffydd (Llywelyn the Last) (d.1282) Prince of Wales. Reigned from *c*.1260 to 1282. The eldest son of Gruffydd, he styled himself 'Prince of Wales' and received recognition from HENRY III of England in 1267. His kingdom embraced Gwynedd, Powys and Deheubarth but after refusing to do homage to EDWARD I in 1276 he lost all his lands except the western part of Gwynedd. His brother provoked another war in 1282 and Llywelyn died in a skirmish at Builth. He was buried at the monastery of Cyn Hir.

Llywelyn ap Iorwerth (Llwelyn the Great) (d.1240) King of Gwynedd. Reigned from 1202 to 1240. He reunited the formerly divided kingdom of Gwynedd in 1202 and came to dominate all other Welsh princes. He successfully evaded the attempts of King JOHN to subdue him and exploited a civil war in England to take control of Powys. He was recognized as Wales's strongest ruler in 1218 and gave himself the title of Lord of Snowdon.

Ludeca King of Mercia. Reigned in 827. An ealdorman who succeeded BEORNWULF, he reigned briefly before being killed in battle along with five of his earls.

Lulach (1032-1058) King of Scots. Reigned from 1057 to 1058. Installed as king on the death of MACBETH, his stepfather. Within seven months he was ambushed and killed by MALCOLM III at Strathbogie. His death was the result of an ongoing dispute as to which branch of the royal line should legitimately hold the throne of Scotland. Lulachs' descendents, including his son Malsnechtai, would continue to challenge the mac-Malcolm dynastys' legitimacy without success for a century.

M

Macbeth (1005-1057) King of Scots. Reigned from 1040 to 1057. A nephew of MALCOLM II, he was one of three kings who came to dominate 11th-century Scotland. He was heriditary *mormaer* (ruler) of Moray, and slew his cousin, King DUNCAN, at Bathgowan, near Elgin, in 1040, and proclaimed himself king. In 1050 he is said to have gone on a pilgrimage to Rome. At the death of their father, the sons of Duncan had taken refuge; Malcolm (later MALCOLM III) with his uncle Siward, Earl of Northumbria, and DONALD Bane in the Hebrides. With Siward's aid, Malcolm invaded Scotland in 1054; a battle was fought at Dunsinane, but it was not until 1057 that Macbeth was finally defeated and slain at Lumphanan in Aberdeenshire. He was married to Gruach, grand-daughter of KENNETH III, and his step-son, LULACH, reigned briefly after his death before being killed by Malcolm who then claimed the throne.

The legends which gradually gathered round the name of Macbeth were collected by John of Fordun and Hector Boece, and reproduced by Holinshed in his *Chronicle*, where they were found by Shakespeare.

Mael Sechnaill I (d.862) High king of Ireland. His reign was threatened in 861 when his rival, AED FINNLIATH, joined with the Norse kings. He survived their attacks but died the following year and Aed became high king.

Mael Sechnaill II (d.1023) High king of Ireland. Reigned from 1002 to 1023 (interrupted). He abdicated in favour of BRIAN BORU in 1014 following his defeat at the Battle of Clontarf. Boru was killed in his tent shortly after the battle however, and he was able to regain the title. Following Mael Sechnaill's death a civil war broke out over the succession and his sons were unable to secure the high kingship. This indirectly ended royal rule in Ireland, as for over 150 years no one could unite the various kingdoms.

Malcolm I (d.954) King of Scots. Reigned from 943 to 954. The son of DONALD II, he succeeded to the throne on the abdication of his cousin CONSTANTINE II. His kingdom was constantly under threat from hostile Norwegian forces both to the north (in Caithness and the Northern Isles under ERIK BLOODAXE) and to the south. He was granted Cumbria by EDMUND in return for recognition of Edmund's sovereignty. He attempted to stamp his authority on the northern lands but without success and was killed in battle by the men of Moray. He was succeeded by his nephew, INDULF.

Malcolm II (*c*.954-1034) King of Scots. Reigned from 1005 to 1034. The son of KENNETH II, he ascended the throne after killing his cousin, KENNETH III, who contested the inheritance, in battle at Monzievaird. On Earl Sigurd of Orkney's death in 1014 at the hands of BRIAN BORU at Clontarf in Ireland, his son Thorfinn became a vassal of Scotland and his lands in Sutherland and Caithness came under Malcolm's control. In the early years of his reign he set about attempting to annexe Bernicia and mounted raids on Northumbria. A victory over the Angles with the assistance of OWEN, king of Strathclyde, at Carham on the Tweed in 1018 secured Lothian as part of Scotland. With Lothian and Strathclyde (probably made a sub-kingdom during Owen's reign) now under his control, Malcolm II had extended his kingdom to include the old lands of Alba and the English speaking lands to the south. When Owen died childless in 1016 Malcolm's grandson, DUNCAN, succeeded him as king of Strathclyde. Malcolm II had no sons and on his death Duncan I became king of all Scotland.

Significant events of Malcolm II's reign

- 1005 – Kenneth III killed at Monzievaird.
- 1014 – Sutherland and Caithness secured as part of Scotland.
- 1016 – Duncan installed as King of Strathclyde.
- 1018 – Battle of Carham secures the Lothians as part of Scotland.

Malcolm III Canmore (1031-1093) King of Scots. Reigned from 1058 to 1093. The 'Canmore' of his title means 'big head' or 'chief'. During the reign of MACBETH, young Malcolm was under the protection of his uncle Siward and spent his early years in exile

in Northumberland. He then visited the court of ED-
WARD THE CONFESSOR and with the English Kings' aid
Malcolm took the Scottish crown with the defeat of
Macbeth at Dunsinane Hill in 1054 and the subsequent killing of both Macbeth (at Lumphanan 1057)
and Macbeth's stepson LULACH, who had assumed
the crown on his stepfathers death. Malcolm married
twice; his first wife, Ingibiorg, widow of Earl
Thorfinn II of Orkney, died in 1069 leaving a son
who would later become DUNCAN II; Malcolm then
married Margaret, sister of the Anglo-Saxon prince
Edgar the Aetheling, who had fled the Norman invasion with her brother. Margaret had six sons by
Malcolm, three of whom would become kings;
EDGAR, ALEXANDER I and DAVID I. Under Margaret's
influence the Scottish court accepted English language and customs as the norm. The queen, an
educated woman and devout Christian, encouraged religious reform and her piety would lead to
her canonisation in 1249.

The king and queen welcomed, and indeed encouraged the influx in refugees from WILLIAM I's regime,
which was a dangerous policy as the Norman king
could see the potential menace of the pretender,
Edgar the Aetheling, to the English throne residing in
a hostile nation whose sister had married its monarch. Malcolm had already made incursions into
Northumbria and Cumbria (in 1069 and in 1070)
when, in 1072, William invaded Scotland. William
forced the Scots king to accept the Treaty of Abernethy whereby Malcolm was obliged to acknowl-

edge the English king as overlord. Malcolm's son
Duncan was taken to England as a hostage. However,
in spite of the treaty, Malcolm once again marched
into England, only to be soundly defeated (1079). In
1091 Malcolm was again forced to submit to an English king, William I's successor WILLIAM Rufus.
Malcolm met his death in an ambush in 1093 on yet
another expedition into England and was not long
survived by his wife Margaret who, already being ill,
died four days after hearing of her husband's death.
Malcolm, buried with his wife at Dunfermline, was
succeeded by his brother DONALD III. His reign began
more than two centuries' almost unbroken rule by the
House of Dunkeld.

Malcolm IV (the Maiden) (1141-1165) King of Scots.
Reigned from 1153 to 1165. The grandson of DAVID I
and eldest of the three sons of Henry, the Earl of
Northumberland. He ascended the throne on David
I's death aged only twelve but had been proclaimed
as heir before David's death and had toured the country to ensure that his succession was acceptable. At
first the kingdom he inherited was peaceful but there
was resentment of David's Normanizing policies and
this carried over into Malcolm's reign. In 1157
HENRY II took back the territories of northern England (Northumberland, Cumberland and
Westmoreland) which had been granted to David I.
Malcolm nevertheless went to France the following
year to fight for Henry (for which he received a
knighthood) and this was taken by many as a sign of
unacceptable subordination. In the west the Lord of

the Isles, SOMERLED, founder of the Macdonald clan, attempted to extend the boundaries of his territory, and sailed up the Clyde, but Malcolm was able to defeat his aggression. To the north the rebellious men of Moray and Galloway were also contained.

Malcolm, surnamed 'the Maiden' because he did not marry, was probably the last Gaelic-speaking monarch. Weakened by the exigences of kingship, he died in his early twenties at Jedburgh Abbey and was succeeded by his younger brother, WILLIAM I (the Lion).

Margaret (Maid of Norway) (1283-90) Queen of Scotland. Reigned from 1286 to 1290. The daughter of Erik II of Norway and Margaret, daughter of ALEXANDER III. Margaret was declared heiress to the Scottish throne in 1284 whilst still an infant, all of her grandfather's other children having died. When Alexander died accidentally two years later Margaret, aged only three, being the sole surviving descendant of the mac-Malcolm line, became queen. The Treaty of Birgham (1290) arranged the marriage of Margaret and Edward of Caenarvon, son and heir of EDWARD I of England, and guaranteed Scotland's separate existence from England, although the two nations were to be jointly ruled. Margaret set sail from Norway in September 1290 but died a short time after reaching Orkney, never having set foot on the Scottish mainland. The Treaty of Birgham was naturally negated by Margaret's death and, with no legitimate successor to the past three generations of Scottish kings, bitter disputes over the succession ensued. During the interregnum the claim to the throne was contested by many 'competitors' the main rivals being JOHN BALLIOL and Robert Bruce, Earl of Annandale. After conferences at Norham and Berwick in 1291, EDWARD I, the English king, found in favour of John Balliol who was crowned king of Scots at Scone in 1292. Margaret was buried at Bergen in the Orkneys.

Mary I (1516-1558) Queen of England and Ireland. Reigned from 1553 to 1558. The only surviving daughter of HENRY VIII by Catherine of Aragon, Mary was declared illegitimate when she was born, but was restored to her rights when the succession was finally settled in 1544. The first undisputed female sovereign of England, she ascended the throne in early 1553, after an abortive attempt to set her aside in favour of LADY JANE GREY. One of her first measures was the reinstatement of the Roman Catholic prelates who had been superseded in the late reign. Her marriage to Philip II of Spain, united as it was with a complete restoration of the Catholic worship, produced much discontent. Insurrections broke out under Cave in Devonshire, and Wyat in Kent, which, although suppressed, formed sufficient excuses for the imprisonment of the Princess ELIZABETH in the Tower, and the execution of Lady Jane Grey and her husband, Lord Guildford Dudley. England was declared to be reconciled to the Pope and the act *De Heretico Comurendo* against heretics was revived. Nearly 300 perished at the stake, including the bishops Cranmer, Latimer, and Ridley. The daily

burnings repulsed the people however, and the martyrs who perished in the fires of Smithfield in London, where most of the burnings were held, secured
the triumph of Protestantism in England.

The people were also angry that England, once a
powerful independent power, appeared to have become little more than a province of Spain. Philip II
dragged England into a war with France which ended
in the humiliating loss of Calais in 1558 after it had
been held by England for over 200 years; and Spain,
with its detested Inquisition, replaced France as the
enemy of the English people. This disgrace told
acutely upon Mary's disordered health, and she died
shortly afterwards. Feasting and dancing in the
streets followed the death of the hated 'Bloody
Mary' and the announcement of the succession of her
Protestant half-sister, Elizabeth.

Significant events of Mary's reign

- 1554 – The announcement of Mary's intention to
         marry Philip II of Spain provokes an
         unsuccessful rebellion.

         Lady Jane Grey and her husband are put
         to death.

         Mary marries Philip II of Spain.

         Mary repeals Edward VI's religious laws
         and the persecution of Protestants begins.

- 1556 – Thomas Cranmer, Archbishop of
         Canterbury, is burned as a heretic.

- 1557 – England enters into war with France.

- 1558 – England loses Calais.

Mary II (1662-1694) Queen of England, Scotland and
Ireland. Reigned from 1689 to 1694. The elder
daughter of James, Duke of York, afterwards JAMES
II, by his wife Anne Hyde, daughter of Lord
Clarendon. Married in 1677 to her cousin WILLIAM,
Prince of Orange. She was a popular princess in Holland and when the Revolution dethroned her father,
she was declared joint-possessor of the throne with
William, on whom all the administration of the government devolved. This unique arrangement lasted
until her death, after which William ruled by himself.

During the absence of William in Ireland in 1690,
and during his various visits to the Continent, Mary
managed at home with extreme prudence and, unlike
her husband, was well-liked by the people. She died
childless and is buried in Westminster Abbey.

Significant events of Mary II's reign

- 1689 – The Toleration Act grants freedom of
  worship to Protestant dissenters.

  A Scottish revolt is crushed.

  A Bill of Rights limits regal power.

  In Ireland Catholic forces loyal to
  James II besiege Londonderry.

- 1690 – James is defeated at the Battle of the
  Boyne.

- 1691 – The Treaty of Limerick allows freedom of
  worship for Catholics.

- 1692 – The Massacre of Glencoe.

- 1694 – The Bank of England is established.

Mary, **Queen of Scots** (1542-1587) Queen of Scotland. Reigned from 1542 to 1567. The ill-fated Mary
Stuart was born at Linlithgow Palace, the daughter of
JAMES V by Mary of Lorraine, a princess of the family of Guise. Her father dying when she was only
seven days old, Mary was crowned at Stirling and the
regency was, after some dispute, vested in the Earl of
Arran (from 1554 in her mother, Mary of Guise). In
1543 the infant was betrothed to the six-year-old
EDWARD, son and heir of HENRY VIII but that agreement was soon repudiated by the Scots. In retaliation
Henry invaded Scotland (1544 and 1545) in what
became known as the 'Rough Wooing', and following the defeat of the Scots at Pinkie his armies occupied large parts of south-eastern Scotland. Mary was
sent to the island priory of Inchmahome for safety
and the Scots asked the French for help. It was duly
given on the condition that Mary be sent to France
and in 1558 she was married to the dauphin, afterwards Francis II.

Mary had made a secret agreement before the marriage, however, that, should she die without issue,
her kingdom should fall to the French Crown. Her
husband died seventeen months after his succession
to the crown, in December 1560, and in the minority
of his brother, Charles IX, power rested with
Catherine de Medici. She was not on very good terms
with Mary, and three years after the accession of
ELIZABETH to the English throne the widowed queen
returned to Scotland.

Mary was heir presumptive to the English Crown,

and Roman Catholics who did not accept the legality of Henry VIII's marriage to Elizabeth's mother, Anne Boleyn, thought that Mary had a better claim to the throne. But when she returned to Scotland she found that the influence of the Presbyterians was paramount in her kingdom. Though inclined to have Roman Catholicism again set up in Scotland, after a vain attempt to influence the leader of the Scottish Reformation, John Knox, she resigned herself to circumstances, quietly allowed her half-brother, the Protestant Earl of Moray, to assume the position of first minister, surrounded herself with a number of other Protestant advisers, and dismissed the greater part of her French courtiers. She even gave these ministers her active support in various measures that had the effect of strengthening the Presbyterian party; but she still continued to have the mass performed in her own private chapel at Holyrood. At first her subjects were quiet, she herself was popular, and her court was one of the most brilliant in Europe.

The calamities of Mary began with her marriage to her cousin, Lord Darnley. He was a Roman Catholic and immediately after the marriage the Earl of Moray and others of the Protestant lords combined against the new order of things. They were compelled to take refuge in England, and the popularity of Mary began to decline. In addition to this; Darnley proved a weak and worthless profligate, and almost entirely alienated the queen by his complicity in the brutal murder of Mary's secretary Rizzio, though a reconciliation seemed to be effected between them about the time of the birth of their son, afterwards JAMES VI of Scotland and I of England in 1556.

About the close of the same year, however, Darnley withdrew from the court, and in the meantime the Earl of Bothwell had risen high in the queen's favour. When the young prince James was baptised at Stirling Castle in December 1566, Bothwell did the honours of the occasion, and Darnley, the father of the prince, was not even present. Once more, however, an apparent reconciliation took place between the king and queen. Darnley had fallen ill, and was lying at Glasgow under the care of his father. Mary visited him, and took measures for his removal to Edinburgh, where he was lodged in a house called Kirk o' Field, close to the city wall. He was there tended by the queen herself but during the absence of Mary at Holyrood the house in which Darnley lay was blown up by gunpowder.

The circumstances attending this crime were very imperfectly investigated, but popular suspicion unequivocally pointed to Bothwell as the ringleader in the outrage, and the queen herself was suspected, suspicion becoming still stronger when she was carried off by Bothwell, with little show of resistance, to his castle of Dunbar, and secretly married to him. A number of the nobles now banded together against Bothwell, who succeeded in collecting a force; but on Carberry Hill, where the armies met, his army melted away. The queen was forced to surrender herself to her insurgent nobles. Bothwell making his escape to Dunbar, then to the Orkney Islands, and finally to Denmark.

The confederates first conveyed the queen to Edinburgh, and thence to Loch Leven Castle, where she was placed in the custody of Lady Douglas, mother of the Earl of Moray. A few days later, a casket containing eight letters and some poetry, all said to be in the handwriting of the Queen fell into the hands of the confederates. The letters, which have come down to us only in the form of a translation, show, if they are genuine, that the writer was herself a party to the murder of Darnley. They were held to afford unmistakable evidence of the queen's guilt, and she was forced to sign a document renouncing the crown of Scotland in favour of her infant son, and appointing the Earl of Moray regent during her son's minority. After remaining nearly a year in captivity Mary succeeded in making her escape from Loch Leven, and, assisted by the few friends who remained loyal to her, made an effort for the recovery of her power.

Defeated by the Regent's forces at the battle of Langside, she fled to England four days later and wrote to Elizabeth entreating protection and a personal interview; but this the later refused to grant until Mary should have cleared herself from the charges laid against her by her subjects. At the end of 1568 commissioners of Elizabeth at York and Westminster heard representatives of Mary and her opponents, with a view as to whether or not she should be restored. No decision was formally made and for one reason or another Elizabeth never granted Mary an interview preferring instead to keep her in more or less close captivity in England, where her life was passed in a succession of intrigues for accomplishing her escape.

For more than eighteen years she continued to be the prisoner of Elizabeth, and in that time the place of her imprisonment was frequently changed, her final prison being Fotheringay Castle, Northamptonshire. During this time there were a series of allegations that she was involved in pro-Catholic plots to depose Elizabeth. She was at last accused of being implicated in the plot by Babington against Elizabeth's life, and having been tried by a court of Elizabeth's appointing was, in late 1586, condemned to be executed. There was a long delay before Elizabeth signed the warrant, but her hand had at last been forced and this was done in February the following year. Mary received the news with great serenity and was beheaded a week later in the castle of Fotheringay.

Authorities are more agreed as to the attractions, talents, and accomplishments of Mary Stuart than as to her character. Contemporary writers who saw her unite in testifying to the beauty of her person, and the fascination of her manners and address. She was witty in conversation, and ready in dispute. In her trial for alleged complicity in Babington's plot she held her ground against the ablest statesman and lawyers of England. She was buried at Peterborough Cathedral until transferred in 1612 by her son to Henry VII's Chapel at Westminster.

Significant events of Mary's reign

- 1548 – Mary is sent to France.
- 1554 – Mary of Guise becomes Regent.
- 1558 – Mary marries the Dauphin Francis
- 1559 – The Scottish Reformation begins with John Knox's return from exile.
    - Mary becomes Queen of France on the accession of her husband (now Francis II of France).
- 1560 – Francis II dies.
- 1561 – Mary returns to Scotland.
- 1565 – Mary marries Lord Darnley, her cousin.
- 1566 – David Rizzio, Mary's secretary, is murdered.
- 1567 – Lord Darnley is murdered.

    Mary is married to the Earl of Bothwell, James Hepburn.

    A rebellion by Scottish lords forces Mary's abdication.

Matilda (Empress Maud) (1102-1167) Queen of England. Reigned in 1141 (uncrowned). The daughter of HENRY I of England and Edith, the daughter of MALCOLM III of Scotland. She was married to Henry V, the Holy Roman Emperor, at the age of twelve and ruled Germany as empress until the death of her husband in 1125. She married Geoffrey Plantagenet of Anjou in 1128 and gave birth to three children including Henry Plantagenet who would later become HENRY II of England.

She was named as heir to the English throne when Henry I's only son, William, met his death on the *White Ship* which was smashed onto rocks when returning to England from Normandy in 1120. Henry I had much persuading to do to make his barons accept his daughter as heir, twice summoning his nobility together to obtain their oath to stand by Matilda. However, the existence of another potential claimant to the throne was to produce complications for the succession. STEPHEN, whose mother Adela of Flanders was the daughter of William the Conqueror and whose father was Stephen of Blois, the leader of the Norman barons with substantial estates in England, believed that he was the rightful male heir, his elder brother having set aside any claim he may have had. On the death of Henry I, Stephen, who had sworn fealty to Matilda along with the rest of the nobility of England, hurried from Blois to claim the throne and, with the aid of his brother Henry, Bishop of Winchester, was installed as king. However, the early support which Stephen had enjoyed soon evaporated when it became clear that he was not as effective at government as Henry I had been. Many barons had wished to increase their power and influence and began to use Stephen's weakness as king to do so, some remembered their sworn allegiance to Matilda. Stephen also began to lose the support of the Church. In 1138 DAVID I of Scotland invaded northern England on Matilda's behalf but was defeated at Northallerton at the Battle of the Standard. Civil war broke out in England soon after. In 1139, while her husband invaded Normandy, Matilda invaded England and was welcomed by a grouping of barons who had switched their support from Stephen, including Robert of Gloucester, an illegitimate son of Henry I who was to prove a useful ally. Matilda set up a base in the west country and at Bristol, Robert of Gloucester's stronghold, and from there further fermented the general rebellion against Stephen's rule. By 1141 the Bishop of Winchester had joined with her cause and in that same year Matilda defeated the kings forces at the Battle of Lincoln and imprisoned Stephen in Bristol Castle. Henry of Winchester proclaimed at a council that divine intervention had indicated God's will that Matilda be queen of England and Normandy. The Queen then travelled to London to claim her crown. However her behaviour when she arrived there did nothing to endear her to the populace of that city. She displayed the fiercely arrogant side of her nature to the Londoners and the nobility, ally or otherwise alike, and imposed a heavy tax on the city. Her falling out with Henry of Winchester led him to abandon her cause and retreat to his palace. Matilda, having come so close to gaining the crown, was chased out, the Londoners demanding Stephen's release. Matilda laid siege to the Bishop of Winchester at Wolvesey Palace, hoping to regain his support by force, but was herself besieged by Stephen's Queen, Matilda of Boulogne. Matilda escaped but Robert of Gloucester was captured; this was a major blow to Matilda's ambitions as Robert was her military leader. King Stephen was released in exchange for Robert but with Stephen restored as king, Matilda's best chance of claiming the throne had passed. The fighting continued but was now more sporadic in nature and gradually diminished in ferocity over the next few years. Matilda was almost captured at her stronghold at Oxford in December 1142 but managed to escape by stealing away into the winter's night, travelling over six miles on foot, in her nightgown, to Wallingford where she obtained a horse. Stephen defeated her forces at the Battle of Farringdon in 1145 but she still fought on, even although her support was growing ever smaller.

The following year Matilda left finally gave up the fight and left England for Normandy which her husband had conquered in her absence. Matilda had failed in her attempt on the English throne but her son, Henry Plantagenet, would be more successful. After invading England in 1153 Henry and King Stephen came to an agreement under which Henry would succeed to the throne on the king's death. Stephen died the following year and Henry II was duly crowned.

N

Nechton (d.*c*.724) King of Picts. Ruled from 706 to 724. The brother of BRIDEI IV, he embraced Christianity and abdicated, leaving four rivals to contest the succession.

Niall of the Nine Hostages (d.405) High king of Ireland. Reigned from 379 to 405. A semi-legendary figure who gained his name by holding nine members of different ruling dynasties hostage at the same time to secure his position as high king. He was succeeded by a son, Loeguire, who controlled much of northern and central Ireland in the year of St Patrick's mission (432). Two of Niall's other sons founded the kingdom of Aileach in 400 which had 52 known sovereigns until 1170.

Nunna King of Sussex. Reigned *c*.710 to c725. He was an under-king of INE of Wessex and participated in his campaign of 710 to bring Kent under his control. He eventually freed his kingdom from subordination and offered refuge to exiles from Wessex. He made land grants to the Bishop of Selsey between 714 and 720 and one of his charters is the first to formally mention Sussex.

O

Octa (d.*c*.540) King of Kent. Reigned from *c*.512 to *c*.540. The grandson of HENGEST, he succeeded his father, AESC.

Oengus (d.761) King of Picts. Reigned from 728 to 761. He claimed the throne during the civil war which erupted after NECHTAN abdicated in 724. He killed his cousin, DREST, one of the four claimants, in 729 and took control of the kingdom of the Dalriadic Scots in 736. He attempted to overrun Strathclyde in 750, but was defeated at Mugdock, near Glasgow. His troubled reign lasted for over thirty years.

Offa (d.*c*.720) King of Essex. Reigned in 709. The son of SIGEHERD, he ruled for less than a year before making a pilgrimage to Rome with Cenred of Mercia and Swafred. He was tonsured and died there after founding a hostel for English pilgrims just outside of Rome.

Offa (d.791) King of Mercia. Reigned from 757 to 796. A descendant of PENDA's younger brother, he defeated his rival claimants to the throne of Mercia in the civil war that followed the death of ETHELBALD.

After an initial period of unrest which saw the Welsh gain territory he established Mercian superiority in all England south of the Humber. Rebellions in Kent led to a ten year period (775-785) in which the independence of that kingdom was re-established. He eventually succeeded in conquering Kent, however, and thereafter it was no more than a province of Mercia. By conquest and marriage he reduced Wessex and East Anglia to almost the same status. He issued the first major royal coinage and built a 120-mile long defensive wall to protect Mercia from Welsh attacks which became known as Offa's Dyke. He was also the first king of Mercia to be recognized as a significant power in Europe and in 789 Charlemagne asked for one of his daughters as a wife for his son. He died at the height of his powers and was succeeded by his son. He had been concerned that the succession would be disputed and had his son, EGFRITH, consecrated as king before his death. Unfortunately his last wish to secure the dynasty was not fulfilled as Egfrtih only outlived his father by a few months.

Olaf I (the White) King of Dublin. Reigned from 853 to c.856. He styled himself 'King of the Northmen of all Ireland and Britain' after uniting all the Viking leaders in 853.

Olaf II (the Red) (b.c.920) King of Dublin. Reigned from c.945 to 980. Following ETHELSTAN's death in 939 he invaded Northumbria and compelled his successor, EDMUND, to cede him lands in the north-east

Midlands known as the Five Boroughs. He also gained land in Bernicia and Edmund had to appeal to the Scots to assist him in keeping Olaf's advances in check. He disputed control of York with his cousin, ERIK BLOODAXE, who was finally driven out by EDRED in 952. He was the longest reigning king of Dublin.

Olaf (Guthfrithson) (d.941) King of Dublin. He was an ally of the Scots under CONSTANTINE II at the Battle of Brunanburgh in 937. He died in an obscure battle whilst raiding lowland Scotland.

Osbald (d.796) King of Northumbria. Reigned in 796. He was one of the conspirators who killed ETHELRED in 796 but only reigned for a few weeks before being ousted by EARDWULF.

Osbert (d.867) King of Northumbria. Reigned from 850 to 865. Expelled in favour of his brother, AELLE. Both were killed in a joint attack on York which had been seized by the Norse while they were fighting over the throne.

Osmund King of Sussex. Reigned from *c.*765 to 770. An under-king of the powerful OFFA of Mercia who annexed the kingdom in 772.

Osred I (d.716) King of Northumbria. Reigned from 705 to 716. The young successor of ALDFRITH in 705, he earned a reputation as a tyrant and was murdered.

Osred II King of Northumbria. Reigned from 788 to 790. A nephew of ELFWOLD, he was imprisoned by ETHELRED I and later escaped to the Isle of Man.

Osric (d.729) King of Northumbria. Reigned from 718 to 729. He was succeeded by his nephew, CEOLWULF.

Oswald (St Oswald) (605-642) King of Northumbria. Reigned from 634 to 642. The brother of ENFRITH, he lived in the Hebrides during EDWIN's reign. On his return he established himself as *Bretwalda*, or over-lord of all the Anglo-Saxon kings, with his victory over Cadwallon of Gwynedd. He then tried to check the advance of Mercia under King PENDA and died fighting him on the Welsh Marches. He was a popular figure and gained the nickname 'Bright Blade' for his abilities in battle. He was also a devout Christian and gave Bishop Aiden the island of Lindisfarne. He was the fist Anglo-Saxon king to be canonized; the 5th of August is his feast day.

Oswin (d.651) King of Deira. Reigned from 642 to 651. The son of OSWALD, he contested the succession with his uncle, OSWY, and took Deira (southern Northumberland) as his kingdom. He was assassinated by his brother at Gilling in 651 and the two kingdoms of Deira and Bernicia were united.

Oswini (d.690) King of Kent. Ruled jointly with from 688 to 690 with SUAEBHARD.

Oswulf (d.759) King of Northumbria. Reigned in 759. The son and successor of EDBERT, he was killed by his own bodyguard within a year of coming to power.

Oswy (602-670) King of Northumbria. Reigned from 651 to 670. The brother of OSWALD, his time as ruler saw the peak of Northumbrian power. After thirteen years ruling Bernicia in MERCIA'S shadow he united his kingdom with Deira by assassinating the ruler, his nephew, OSWIN at Gilling. He went on to defeat and kill the powerful King PENDA of Mercia and many of his under-kings in 655 on the flooded River Winwaed (near Leeds) to become *Bretwalda*, or overlord of all Anglo-Saxon kings. He also contributed to the development of religion in England by presiding over the Synod at Whitby in 664 which resolved many of the disputes between the Celtic and Roman Churches. His daughter Alchfled married PEADA of Mercia only after he was persuaded to convert to Christianity.

Owain Gwynedd (1100-1170) King of Gwynedd. Reigned from 1137 to 1170. He united the kings in the south to resist HENRY II's advances into Wales in 1165. His son married Henry's illegitimate half-sister. He is buried in Bangor Cathedral.

Owen (the Bald) (d.*c.*1018) King of Strathclyde. Probably the last king of Strathclyde. An ally of King MALCOLM II of Scotland, he helped defeat Earl Uhtred of Northumbria at the Battle of Carham on the river Tweed (1018). It is thought that by this time Strathclyde was a sub-kingdom of Scotland and Owen only a vassal king.

P

Peada (d.656) King of Middle Anglia. Reigned from 653 to 656. The youngest son of PENDA, he was made an under-king of Middle Anglia, a kingdom created by his father in 653. He married Alchfled, the daughter of Oswy of Bernicia, who slew his father Penda in 655. Oswy gave Peada his daughter on the condition that he be converted to Christianity. In Bede's *Historia Ecclesiastica* it is claimed that Peada was murdered through the treachery of his wife.

Penda (577-655) King of Mercia. Reigned from 626 to 655. The son of PYBBA, this pagan king established Mercian supremacy by defeating the West Saxons at Cirencester in 628 and the then all-powerful EDWIN of Northumbria in 633 at Heathfield in Yorkshire with the help of CADWALLON of Gwynedd. It was under Penda that the Mercians evolved from being a tribe to being a powerful people and a formidable enemy. Penda's policy as king was to maintain the independence of his kingdom from Northumbrian domination. This led him to make two very destructive attacks on Northumbria as Oswy of Bernicia attempted to reunite the kingdom. He was finally defeated and killed during his last invasion at the battle on the flooded river at Winwaed by the much smaller army of Oswy. He features heavily in Bede's *Ecclesiastical History* where he is portrayed as an anti-hero pagan warrior-king.

Prasutagus (d.60) King of the Iceni. He ruled the tribal kingdom as a client of the Romans but when he died his lands were seized, his daughters raped and his wife, BOADICEA, flogged. Boadicea led a rebellion which was eventually quashed.

Pybba (d.c.606) King of Mercia. Reigned from c.593 to c.606. He is thought to have been the son of CREODA, the first king of the Mercians. His family of three sons and two daughters founded the Mercian dynasty.

R

Redwald King of East Anglia. He reigned from *c.*593 to *c.*617 and was considered to be *Bretwalda*, overlord of all Anglo-Saxon king in England. He helped EDWIN win the Northumbrian throne in 617 by defeating and killing ETHELFRITH at a battle on the River Idle on the Deiran frontier. He converted to Christianity but lapsed back to paganism, supposedly by his wife. The pagan ship burial site at Sutton Hoo near Ipswich is thought to commemorate his death.

Rhodi Mawr (the Great) King of Gwynedd. Reigned from 844 to 878. He resisted several attacks by the Vikings and came to dominate Powys and Deheubarth in south Wales. He was eventually forced into exile in Ireland by the Vikings and killed in battle by a Mercian army on his return.

Richard (I) the Lionheart (1157-1199) King of England. Reigned from 1189 to 1199. The third son of HENRY II by Eleanor of Aquitaine, he was born at Beaumont Palace, Oxford. In his youth, as Duke of Aquitaine, Richard rebelled against his father, at length fighting alongside Philip II of France. On Henry's death at Chinon, Richard sailed to England where he was crowned at Westminster Abbey. Very much a warrior king, Richard spent only six months of his reign in England and the principal events of his reign are connected with the third Crusade against Muslim rule in the Holy Land in which he took part, uniting his forces with those of Philip of France. In the course of this Crusade he conquered Cyprus, retook Acre and Jaffa and married the Princess Berengaria of Navarre whilst in Cyprus. He failed to take Jerusalem from Saladin but secured access for Christians to the Holy places.

Richard left Palestine in 1192 and sailed for the Adriatic but was wrecked near Aguileia. On his way home through Germany he was seized by the Duke of Austria (in spite of his disguise as a woodsman) whom he had offended in Palestine, and was given up a prisoner to the Emperor Henry VI. During his seventeen month captivity his brother, John, headed an insurrection, which was suppressed by Richard when he returned to England in 1194 after the ransom securing his release was paid (an unlikely legend tells of Richard being found by his favourite minstrel, Blondel, who sang under the walls of each castle he passed on his way back from the Crusades to England).

Richard spent the rest of his life in Normandy fighting Philip II of France. He died of a shoulder wound received whilst besieging the castle of Châlus. Legend has it that he pardoned the archer who fired the arrow which killed him. Richard, although utterly neglectful of his duties as a king, was a popular figure who owed his fame chiefly to his abilities as a military leader and to his personal bravery.

Significant events of Richard I's reign

- 1189 – The Third Crusade is launched.

- 1191 – Richard conquers Cyprus but fails to capture Jerusalem.

- 1192 – Richard captures Jaffa and makes peace with Saladin.

   Richard is captured by Duke Leopold of Austria.

- 1194 – A ransom is paid and Richard travels to England.

   Richard leaves England once more to fight Philip II of France.

- 1199 – Richard lays siege to Chalus Castle.

Richard II (1367-1400) King of England and Wales. Reigned from 1377 to 1399. The second and only surviving son of Edward the Black Prince and Joan of Kent and the grandson of EDWARD III. He was born at Bordeaux, succeeded his grandfather at the age of ten, and was crowned at Westminster Abbey. In the years of Richard's minority the government was in the hands of his uncles, firstly John of Gaunt and later Thomas of Gloucester.

These were troubled times; the continuing cost of the Hundred Years' War (1337-1453), the aftermath of the Black death and John of Gaunt's misrule culminated in the Peasants Revolt of 1381. The insurrection, led by Wat Tyler at the head of upwards of

10,000 men, was a reaction the imposition of a poll
tax which weighed heavily on the poor whose wages
were being held down by legislation (the Statute of
Labourers, 1351, held wages and prices at 1340's
levels). First introduced in 1377 and again in 1379, a
higher tax was imposed in 1380 with officials being
sent into the country to collect arrears; violence
against the tax collectors became common. On the
13th of June 1381 Tyler and his men had reached
London, leaving in their wake a trail of destruction,
and made their demands of the king, which included
the abolishment of serfdom and a pardon for all who
had taken part in the rebellion. The young Richard
agreed to these demands but, after the danger had
passed, his government reneged on the agreement
and almost two hundred peasant were killed in the reprisals which followed. However, once the unpopular poll tax was abolished Richard found the revolts
of his nobles more difficult to contain. The Lords
Appellant, under the Duke of Gloucester, rebelled
against the unpopular government of John of Gaunt
and seized control in 1387; many of Richard's advisers and personal friends were killed or banished. The
Lords Appellant ruled until 1389 when the king, having reached his majority, took over the reigns of
power. Richard's revenge was exacted in 1397 with
killing or banishment of the Lords Appellant, including the exile of Henry of Bolingbroke. John of
Gaunt, the Duke of Lancaster, died in 1399 and his
estates were confiscated by the king. These acts of
despotism infuriated many of the nobles and in that

same year, whilst Richard was in Ireland attempting to subdue the western part of the country, Henry of Bolingbroke (now Duke of Lancaster on John of Gaunt's death) landed in England and claimed the throne. Parliament accused Richard of having violated his coronation oaths and he was deposed in favour of Bolingbroke. Thus the Commons became little more than a pawn in the hands of rival court factions.

The deposed king was imprisoned at Pontefract Castle where he died the following year, either being murdered or starving himself to death. Richard was married twice, firstly to Anne of Bohemia, daughter of Emperor Charles IV, in 1382 (died 1394) and then to Isabella of France, daughter of King Charles VI of France, in 1396 (opposed by the Duke of Gloucester) but neither of the marriages produced children. Something of a tyrant, Richard was nonetheless a feeble ruler who was unable to stamp his royal authority on the kingdom. A lover of the arts, Richard took a particular interest in literature and patronized Geoffrey Chaucer. He has also been credited with conceiving the handkerchief. He was buried at Kings Langley, Hertfordshire and reburied at Westminster Abbey in 1413.

Significant events of Richard II's reign

- 1381 – The Peasants' revolt.
- 1389 – The Lords Appellant seize power.

  Richard assumes control of government.
- 1394 – Richard attempts to conquer the west of Ireland.

- 1397 – Reprisals are taken against the Lords
  Appellant and Bolingbroke is expelled.

  Chaucer writes *The Canterbury Tales*.

- 1398 – Richard assumes absolute rule.

- 1399 – Duke of Lancaster deposes Richard with
  the approval of Parliament.

Richard III (1452-1485) King of England and Wales.
Reigned from 1483 to 1485. The last of the Yorkist
kings was the youngest son of Richard Plantagenet,
Duke of York, and Lady Cecily Neville. On the accession of his brother, EDWARD IV, he was created
Duke of Gloucester, and during the early part of
Edward's reign served him with great courage and fidelity, taking part in the battles of 1471 against the
Lancastrian supporters of HENRY VI, the rival to
Edward's throne. Marriage to Anne Neville, joint-
heiress of the Earl of Warwick, brought him great
wealth, although disputes over the inherited estates
also caused friction between himself and his younger
brother, the Duke of Clarence, who married Anne's
sister.

From 1480 to 1482 Richard was Lieutenant General in the North where he won acclaim for his successes over the Scots at Edinburgh and Berwick. On
the death of Edward he was appointed as Protector of
the Kingdom and his nephew, the young EDWARD V,
was declared king. Richard swore fealty to the king
but soon began to pursue his own ambitious
schemes. The young king had grown up under the
guidance of the powerful Woodville family and

Richard had never been on good terms with them since he had objected to the marriage of Edward IV to Elizabeth. Before the coronation could take place, therefore, he moved against the leading members of the family. Earl Rivers, the queen's brother, and Sir Robert Grey, a son by her first husband, were arrested and beheaded at Pomfret. Lord Hastings, who was faithful to his young sovereign, was executed without trial in the Tower. With the support of the Bishop of Bath and Wells he then declared that the king and his brother were illegitimate, as their father had been betrothed to another before he married their mother, and that he, as a result, had a legal title to the crown. The Duke of Buckingham supported Richard, and Parliament had little choice but to offer him the crown. The deposed king and his brother were, according to general belief, smothered in the Tower of London by order of their uncle. The Duke of Buckingham later revolted against Richard but this came to nothing as the rebellion was crushed and Buckingham beheaded.

Richard governed with vigour and ability and set about making financial and legal reforms, but was not generally popular and faced increasing opposition to his slight claim to kingship. In 1485 HENRY Tudor, Earl of Richmond, head of the House of Lancaster and rival claimant to the throne, landed with a small army at Milford Haven in West Wales and soon gathered support from the disaffected nobility. Richard met him with an army of 8,000 men at Bosworth in Leicestershire. Richmond's force was initially smaller, but Lord Stanley and Sir William Stanley joined with the Lancastrians and enabled him to win a decisive victory. Richard wore his crown on the field and is said to have come within a sword's length of Henry before being cut down. His body was subjected to indignities and afterwards buried in Leicester. Henry was crowned on the field. The Wars of the Roses were at last over, and the two warring Houses united by the marriage of Henry VII to Edward IV's daughter, Elizabeth. The reconciliation was symbolized by the red and white rose of the House of Tudor.

Richard possessed courage as well as capacity; but his conduct showed cruelty, treachery, and ambition. His personal defects were no doubt magnified by the character assassinations of historians loyal to the House of Tudor, but he remains one of the most maligned of English kings. Contrary to Shakespeare's portrayal, there is no evidence that he was a hunchback. He is buried at the Abbey of the Grey Friars in Leicester.

Significant events of Richard III's reign

- 1483 – Edward V and his brother are murdered in the Tower.

  Buckingham's rebellion is crushed.

  The College of Arms, which regulates the issue of coats of arms, is established.

- 1484 – William Caxton prints *Morte D'Arthur*.

  The Council of the North is established to govern the north of England.

- 1484   Bail for defendants in legal courts is
          introduced.

          English is used for the first time for
          Parliamentary statutes.

- 1485 – Richard III killed in the Battle of
          Bosworth.

Robert (I) the Bruce (1274-1329) King of Scots. Considered to be the greatest of the Scottish kings, Robert de Bruce VIII was born in Essex, and as the second Earl of Carrick, swore fealty to EDWARD I. In 1297 he fought with the English against William Wallace before joining the Scots in their fight for independence. He briefly returned to his allegiance with Edward until 1298, when he again joined the national party, and became in 1299 one of the four regents of the kingdom.

In the three final campaigns, however, he resumed fidelity to Edward, and resided for some time at his Court; but, learning that the king meditated putting him to death on information given by the traitor Comyn (a rival for the Scottish throne), he fled to Scotland, stabbed Comyn in a quarrel at Dumfries, assembled his vassals at Lochmaben Castle, and claimed the crown, which he received at Scone. Being twice defeated by the English, he dismissed his troops, retired to Rathlin Island, and was supposed to be dead, when, in the spring of 1307, he landed on the Carrick coast, defeated the Earl of Pembroke at Loudon Hill, and in two years had wrested nearly the whole country from the English. He then in successive years advanced into England, laying waste the country, and, in 1314, defeated at Bannockburn the English forces advancing under EDWARD II to the relief of the garrison at Stirling. (The Monymusk Reliquary, used by KENNETH MAC-ALPIN to carry St Columba's relics from Iona to Dunkeld, legend has it, was carried into battle at Bannockburn). He then went to Ireland to the aid of his brother EDWARD, and on his return in 1318, in retaliation for inroads made during his absence, took Berwick and harried Northumberland and Yorkshire.

In the face of continuing English aggression, 31 lords and earls met at Arbroath Abbey and wrote to Pope John XXII seeking recognition of Scotland as a sovereign state independent of England (the Declaration of Arbroath, or sometimes called the Declaration of Independence). Hostilities continued until the defeat of Edward near Byland Abbey in 1323, and though in that year a truce was concluded for thirteen years, it was speedily broken. Not until 1328 was the treaty concluded by which the independence of Scotland was fully recognized (the Treaty of Northampton).

Bruce did not long survive the completion of his work, dying the following year at Cardross Castle. His heart was buried at Melrose Abbey and his other remains at Dunfermline. He was twice married; first to a daughter of the Earl of Mar, Isabella, by whom he had a daughter, Marjory, mother of ROBERT II; and then to a daughter of Aymer de Burgh, Earl of Ulster, Elizabeth, by whom he had a son, DAVID, who succeeded him.

Significant events of Robert I's reign

- 1306 – Bruce forced to flee Edward I's army.
- 1307 – Edward I dies on his way to Scotland.
- 1314 – The Battle of Bannockburn.
- 1315 – Robert's brother, Edward Bruce, is crowned as High king of Ireland.
- 1320 – The Declaration of Arbroath is drawn up and dispatched to the Pope.
- 1323 – Bruce enters into a truce with the English.
- 1327 – Edward III becomes King of England.
- 1328 – The Treaty of Northampton acknowledges the independence of Scotland.

Robert II (1316-1390) King of Scots. Reigned from 1371 to 1390. The son of Marjory, daughter of ROBERT Bruce, and of Walter, Steward of Scotland, Robert II was the first of the Steward (later changed to Stuart) kings. During DAVID II's period of imprisonment in England, 'Auld Blearie', as he was known on account of his bloodshot eyes, had acted as regent, having been recognized by Parliament in 1318 as heir to the throne. On David II's death he was crowned at Scone. He was married twice, firstly to Elizabeth Mure (1348) who bore him nine children before marriage, and secondly, on Elizabeth's death, to Euphemia Ross who bore him four children. An Act of Parliament in 1375 settled the crown on his sons by his first wife, Elizabeth, illegitimate by ecclesiastical law. A feeble king, Robert effectively handed over power to his eldest son, John, Earl of Carrick (later ROBERT III). His reign was comparatively a peaceful one, one of the chief events being the defeat of the English at the Battle of Otterburn in 1388.

Robert III (1337-1406) King of Scots. Reigned from 1390 to 1406. The eldest son of ROBERT II and Elizabeth Mure. He was originally called John, but changed his name on his coronation in 1390. Having been crippled by being kicked by a horse, he was unable to engage in military pursuits, and he trusted the management of government affairs almost entirely to his brother, whom he created Duke of Albany. In 1398 Albany was compelled to resign his office by a party who wished to confer it on the king's eldest son, David, Duke of Rothesay. War was renewed with England in 1402 and an extended raid reached as far as Newcastle but the Battle of Homildon Hill resulted in a crushing defeat for the Scots. In this year the Duke of Rothesay died in Falkland Castle, where he had been imprisoned, commonly believed to have been starved to death at the instigation of Albany. Dread of Albany, who had recovered the regency, induced the king to send his second son, JAMES, to France in 1406; but the ship which carried him was captured by the English, and HENRY IV detained him as a prisoner for the next 18 years. Shortly after hearing of his son's capture Robert III died heartbroken. He was succeeded by his son James I.

Rory O'Connel (d.1198) High king of Ireland. Reigned from 1116 to 1186. He sought Anglo-Norman assistance in his fight to take control of Leinster in 1169. An invasion by Richard de Clare, the Earl of Pembroke, followed in which Wexford, Waterford and Dublin were captured for England. In 1171 HENRY II landed near Waterford to assert his crown rights and receive homage from the native kings; O'Connel recognized Henry as his overlord in 1175.

Run (d.*c*.878) King of Strathclyde. He married a daughter of KENNETH mac-Alpin, the Scots king, and their son, EOCHA, followed CONSTANTINE and AED to the throne, thus strengthening ties between the Scots and Britons of Strathclyde.

S

Saebert (d.606) King of Essex. Reigned from 605 to 616. An early convert to Christianity, he established a bishopric in London in 605. He was succeeded by his sons, SEXRED and SAEWARD.

Saelred (d.746) King of Essex. Reigned from 709 to 746. He was descended from SIGEBERHT the Good. Little is known of him other than that he died a violent death.

Saeward (d.616) King of Essex. Reigned in 616. The son of SAEBERT, he reigned briefly with his brother, SEXRED. After reverting to paganism the brothers expelled Bishop Mellitus from London and were both killed by the West Saxons as a result.

Sebbi King of Essex. Reigned from 665 to 695. A joint ruler with his nephew SIGHERE, he abdicated to take monastic vows in London and is buried at Old St Paul's.

Sexred (d.616) King of Essex. Reigned in 616. The son of SAEBERT, he reigned jointly with his brother, SAEWARD. Both were killed by the West Saxons after expelling Bishop Mellitus from London.

Sigeberht (d.*c.*634) King of East Anglia. Reined from 631 to 634. A half-brother of EORPWALD, he founded the bishopric of Dunwich for St Felix. He also built the monastery at Burgh Castle on the site of a Roman fort.

Sigeberht (d.759) King of Wessex. Reigned from 756 to 757. He was deposed by the council of kings and ealdormen (the *Witan*) and exiled by CYNEWULF who was elected in his place. He was murdered in revenge for the killing of one of Cynewulf's supporters.

Sigeberht I (the Little) (d.653) King of Essex. Reigned from 617 to 653. Succeeded by his son, also SIGEBERHT.

Sigeberht II (the Good) King of Essex. Reigned from 653 to 660. After his baptism he restored Christianity to the kingdom after a generation of paganism.

Sigered (d.825) King of Essex. Reigned from 798 to 825. The last king of Essex before the kingdom became absorbed by Wessex.

Sigeric King of Essex. Reigned from 758 to 798. Ruled as an under-king of Mercia before abdicating.

Sigeherd (d.*c.*709) King of Essex. Reigned from 695 to 709. Succeeded his father SEBBI and became joint ruler with his brother, SWALFRED.

Sighere (d.*c.*695) King of Essex. Reigned from 665 to 695. Son of SWITHELM, he shared the throne with his uncle, SEBBI. He married a Mercian princess.

Sledda (d.*c.*605) King of Essex. Reigned from 587 to 605. He married a sister of Ethelbert I of Kent.

Somerled (d.1164) King of (the Isle of) Man. Reigned from 1158 to 1164. He was the seventh king of Man and became the first Lord of the Isles after expelling the Norsemen in 1140. His nine male descendants claimed the Hebrides until 1493 and he is considered to be the founder of the powerful MacDonald clan.

Stephen (1096-1154) King of England. Reigned from 1135 to 1154. The son of Stephen, Count of Blois, and Adela, daughter of WILLIAM the Conqueror. He went to the court of HENRY I (his uncle) in 1114 and received the courtship of Mortain in Normandy. Despite having sworn fealty to the Empress Maud (MATILDA) when she was named as heir, he was persuaded to claim the throne on Henry's death. After convincing the Archbishop of Canterbury that he was the legitimate heir and that he had King Henry's approval he was duly crowned king of England in 1135. However, there was some rancour from Maud's supporters and several years of unrest ensued. Many barons had sworn fealty to the Empress and some had become disillusioned with Stephen because his leadership was neither as effective nor as strong as Henry I's had been. An invasion of the north of England was undertaken by King DAVID of Scotland on Maud's behalf (1138) but the Scots were crushed near Northallerton at the Battle of the Standard (Scotland, however, retained Cumberland). The rebelliousness of his barons was more difficult to deal with; Robert, Earl of Gloucester, an illegitimate son of Henry I, had attended Stephen's court in early 1136 but now turned against him, and several nobles, such as the

Earl of Chester, were only too willing to exploit the weakness of the king and the divisions in the country to enhance their own power and standing.

Stephen had not shown himself able to deal decisively with insurrection thus far and this would not change with the coming of his rival for the throne. In September 1139 Maud arrived in England, landing at Arundel, and was welcomed by a group of barons, including the Earl of Gloucester, and with their aid she secured a base in the west country and rallied all those disillusioned with Stephen's reign. Stephen was defeated at the battle of Lincoln (1141) and imprisoned. The Empress proceeded to London but, when the Londoners called for Stephen's release and rose against her, she was forced to flee . She fled to Winchester but was besieged there by an army raised by Stephen's queen, Matilda of Boulogne. Maud escaped but Robert of Gloucester, who had become central to the campaign, was captured. Stephen regained his liberty, being exchanged in return for Robert, and he returned to the throne.

The following years saw sporadic outbreaks of warfare between the rival factions, with Stephen almost capturing Maud in her stronghold at Oxford (1142), but the fighting gradually decreased in intensity until 1148 when Maud returned to Normandy. She had, however, laid the foundations for a successful claim by her son and his descendants. The dispute over the kingship of England continued and HENRY, eldest son of Maud and one day to become Henry II of England, made his third and most successful invasion of England in 1153 backed by a sizeable army. Stephen fought against him but, with the intervention of the church who wished to see peace and stability restored, a compromise was reached. It was arranged that Stephen should remain king until his death and thereafter Henry would ascend the throne. Stephen died the following year (1154), never having been able to stamp his authority on the realm or bring his wayward barons to heel. Henry II was duly crowned King of England, the first of the Plantagenet kings.

Significant events of Stephen's reign

- 1135 – Stephen becomes King of England.
- 1136 – Stephen subdues baronial revolts.
- 1138 – The Earl of Gloucester defects to Matilda's camp.

    David I of Scotland invades northern England in support of Matilda.

    David loses the Battle of the Standard.
- 1139 – Matilda lands in England.
- 1141 – Stephen is captured at the Battle of Lincoln and is imprisoned.

    Matilda claims the throne.

    Robert of Gloucester is captured and exchanged for the King.
- 1142 – Matilda is besieged at Oxford but escapes.
- 1147 – Robert of Gloucester dies.

    Henry (later Henry II) unsuccessfully claims the throne.

- 1148 – Matilda leaves for Normandy.
- 1149 – Henry attempts to take the throne for the second time.
- 1151 – Henry becomes Count of Anjou on the death of his father.
- 1153 – Treaty of Westminster agrees that Henry will become king on Stephen's death.

Suaebhard (d.692) King of Kent. Reigned from 690 to 692. Joint ruler with WIHTRED.

Swalfred (d.c.712) King of Essex. Reigned from 695 to 709. Succeeded his father, SEBBI, and ruled jointly with his brother, SIGEHERD. With his nephew, OFFA, he visited Rome in 709.

Sweyn Forkbeard (d.1014) King of England, Norway and Demark. Reigned (England) from 1013 to 1014. The son of Harold Bluetooth of Denmark and Queen Gunild, he built his North Sea empire through conquest and marriage. In 978 he seized his father's kingdom of Denmark and began making raids on England, often demanding protection payments. In 1000 he attacked Norway and became ruler. Two years later ETHELRED, the king of England, fearing that Sweyn's empire would overrun his kingdom, ordered that the Danes settled in England be massacred. This order was impracticable in many areas where the Danes had strongholds but where the policy was carried out the consequences were terrible. Among the Danes massacred at Oxford was Sweyn's sister, Gunnhild, and Sweyn's resolve to rule England was hardened. The Massacre of St Brice's Day turned support from Ethelred and the king executed many who expressed pro-Danish sympathies. Sweyn enjoyed several early successes at Oxford and Winchester but was unable to seize London despite frequent attempts in 994. By late 1013, however, he had devastated fifteen counties and driven Ethelred from England. He was accepted soon after as king of England but died early the next year following a fall from his horse. He had two sons; Harold IV of Denmark and CANUTE, later to be king of England.

Swithhelm (d.665) King of Essex. Reigned from 660 to 665. He was baptised by St Cedd although his kingdom lapsed back to paganism following the arrival of a plague in 664. Succeeded by his son, SEBBI and his brother, SIGHERE, who ruled jointly.

Swithred King of Essex. Reigned from 746 to 758. He made Colchester the capital of his kingdom.

T

Talorcen (d.657) King of Picts. The son of EANFRITH of Bernicia.

Talorgen (d.787) King of Picts. He reigned from 785 to 787.

Tincommius (*fl.*15) King of the Atrebates tribe. One of COMMIUS's three sons who divided their father's kingdom and used the title of *Rex*, meaning 'king'. He was recognized by Augustus around 15 BC.

Togodummus (*fl.*50) High king of British tribes. Son of CUNOBELINUS and brother of CARADOC, he resisted the Romans and was probably killed at the Battle of the Medway.

Tytila (d.*c.*593) King of East Anglia. Reigned from *c.*578 to *c.*593. The successor of WUFFA.

U

Uen (d.c839) King of Picts. Reigned from 837 to 839. Frequent attacks by the Norse, which claimed Uen, indirectly led to the unification of Pictland and Dalriada. Uen's brothers were also killed, as were most of the members of the major families of the Pictish kingdom, leaving a power vacuum which KENNETH MAC-ALPIN was later able to exploit to become king of both Picts and Scots.

Unuist King of Picts. The brother of DREST IV, reigned from 820 to 834.

Urien King of Rheged. A British king, descended from King COEL, who ruled this kingdom around the Solway Firth in the late 5th century. One of the last rulers, he fought the Bernicians who sought to move north and west from the Humber. The poem *Gododdin* describes one such Bernician attack at Catterick. There is evidence that Urien also allied with Strathclyde. He was assassinated by a rival tribal chief.

Uurad (d.842) King of Picts. Reigned from 839 to 842. Four of his sons claimed the throne after him.

V

Victoria (1819-1901) Queen of the United Kingdom of Great Britain and Ireland; from 1876 Empress of India. Reigned from 1837 to 1901. The only child of Edward, Duke of Kent, fourth son of GEORGE III, by his wife, Mary Louisa Victoria, daughter of Francis, Duke of Saxe-Coburg, and widow of Ernest, Prince of Leiningen, was born at Kensington Palace, London. Her prospect of the succession to the crown was somewhat remote, for her father might reasonably hope for a male heir; his three elder brothers were alive, and one of them, the Duke of Clarence, afterwards WILLIAM IV, had recently married. The deaths of the princess's father in 1820 and of her cousins, two daughters of the Duke of Clarence, in 1819–20, placed her next in the succession to her two elderly uncles, the Dukes of York and Clarence. The Duke of York died in 1827, and on the accession of William IV in 1830 Victoria became heiress-presumptive to the throne.

She had been brought up very quietly, but from 1830 she began to make public appearances, to the annoyance of King William, who was on very bad terms with the Duchess of Kent. Her coming-of-age, on her eighteenth birthday, was the occasion of some public rejoicings, and when she succeeded her uncle later that year, created a most favourable impression by the tact and composure which she displayed in difficult circumstances. Her accession involved the separation of the crowns of Great Britain and Hanover, the latter passing to the nearest male heir, her uncle, the Duke of Cumberland. In the first years of her reign, Queen Victoria was under the guidance of her Whig Prime Minister, Lord Melbourne, who devoted himself to the task of training a young girl for her high responsibilities and encouraging her to involve herself in official business. Lord Melbourne and Victoria developed an affectionate relationship, so much so that there were fears that the young queen may become to closely associated with the Whig party. The General Election, which by the then existing law followed her accession, gave the Whigs a reduced but adequate majority; but in the summer of 1839 Melbourne's position in the Commons became so weak that he resigned, and the young queen encountered her first political difficulties in a controversy with Sir Robert Peel who, in taking office, proposed to replace the some of the Whig Ladies of the Bedchamber by Conservatives. On her refusal, Peel declined to take office, and Melbourne returned to power for two more years; but the queen, who was taken by surprise and given insufficient time for consideration, afterwards admitted that she had been 'foolish', and no similar difficulty arose again.

The influence of Melbourne diminished after the

queen's marriage in 1840 to her cousin, Prince Albert of Saxe-Coburg, whose wide interests and sagacious counsel had an important effect upon the development of the queen's character, though he never acquired popularity in his adopted country. Their first child, Victoria, afterwards the Empress Frederick, the Queen's favourite child, with whom Queen Victoria would correspond on an almost daily basis for more than forty years following 'Vicky's' marriage to the Crown Prince of Prussia in 1858, was born later the same year, and the Prince of Wales (EDWARD VII) the following year; seven other children followed between 1843 and 1857. Queen Victoria reigned during a period of tremendous change both at home and abroad. Conditions for the poor in the industrial north of the country were growing worse due to economic depression and calls for political change were voiced by the Chartists whose demands included universal male suffrage and secret ballots and opposition to the Corn Laws of 1815, which kept the price of bread high by banning cheap imports of corn, rumbled on. The Corn Laws were finally repealed in 1846 but the Chartist demonstration of 1848, the year of revolutions all over Europe, achieved little. The industrialisation of Britain moved on apace and the Great Exhibition of 1851, conceived by Prince Albert, showcased over 100,000 industrial products by more than 13,000 exhibitors, over half of which were British, at the purpose built Crystal Palace in London.

Britain's Empire grew considerably during Victoria's reign; at the height of its expansion the Union Jack flew over one quarter of the world's land surface, taking in Australia, New Zealand, Canada, many colonies in Africa and the far east and the Indian sub-continent. In India, which had been under the administration of the East India Company with limited supervision from the British government since 1600, a native uprising was to have a profound effect on the development of Britain as an Imperial Power. The East India Company's army in Bengal was an undisciplined unit; grievances over pay, disputes between officers of different castes and rumours that the Government wished to convert India to Christianity by force were among the causes of general unrest and the court-martial of Indian troopers at Meerut in the spring of 1857 (they had refused to touch munitions which they believed had been greased with the fat of pigs and cows) and their subsequently being stripped of their uniforms turned into a mutiny later that year. Three regiments of sepoys (Indian soldiers) freed the prisoners after murdering their guards and marched on Delhi and, once there, killed every European in sight. The mutiny spread like wildfire; the worst excesses were perpetrated at Cawnpore where over 900 British and loyal Indians, men, women and children, were slaughtered. At length the revolt was overcome and Delhi re-taken. The government of India was passed to the British Crown who promised equality and freedom of worship for all. The government which replaced the East India Company was detached from those it ruled with an efficiency and impartiality that would become the model for the rest of the empire's colonies.

Victoria came to be regarded as the figurehead for all of Britain's possessions overseas. She played a considerable part in foreign policy, and on several occasions her personal intervention improved foreign relations, especially with France. No sovereign of this country had left the island since GEORGE II (except for the brief visit of GEORGE IV to Hanover), but Queen Victoria made royal visits a part of the peace-loving diplomacy of her Governments, and she paid special attention both to Louis Philippe and Napoleon III, who owed to her his reception into the royal circles of Europe. Her relations with her ministers during this period were generally cordial, though she had grave disagreements with Palmerston, whose foreign policy she distrusted and whose blunt and bullishly worded despatches to British Ambassadors overseas, sent without her consultation, she resented. Victoria considered the possibilities of dismissing Palmerston but settled instead on the assurance that any such despatches should first be approved by her. Her desire for the maintenance of peace and her frequent correspondence with the Czar, which was of great help to her government, nevertheless led, just before the outbreak of the Crimean War (1854-56), to many misrepresentations of her attitude, which was supposed to be too friendly to Russia. The Queen also displayed a great fondness for Scotland and made two visits there, in 1842 and again in 1844, and oversaw the rebuilding of Balmoral Castle in Speyside, which was her favourite home.

The death of her husband (who in 1857 had been created Prince Consort) from typhoid fever in 1861 changed the whole tenor of the queen's life. Victoria was to wear the black of mourning for the rest of her days and during many years of her widowhood, she lived in almost complete seclusion. She had been the first sovereign to reside in Buckingham Palace, but after 1861 she was rarely in London and preferred Balmoral and Osborne (her home in the Isle of Wight) to Windsor, and her disinclination to appear in public was the subject of numerous complaints.

Her devotion to the other duties was, however, undiminished. She continued to exercise some influence on foreign policy, and advocated neutrality in the Danish War of 1864. She was on terms of intimate friendship with one of the Prime Ministers of this period of her reign, Disraeli, and his Royal Titles Act of 1876, which conferred on her the dignity of Empress of India, gave her special pleasure. She did not like W.E. Gladstone, and did not conceal her reluctance to ask him to form a government in 1880, and her distrust of his policy was increased by the course of events in Egypt and the Sudan. In the last years of her reign she welcomed the Unionist administrations of 1886 and 1890.

Queen Victoria suffered many family griefs, for two of her children and several of her grandchildren predeceased her. She felt deeply the loss of her son-in-law, the Emperor Frederick, in 1888. She had watched with anxiety the aggressive policy of Germany and Bismarck, and had warned her daughter that this country 'cannot and will not stand' the attempt of the German Empire 'to dictate to Europe', and she trusted that her son-in-law's succession would produce a change in German policy. However, by the end of the century Germany had begun arming rapidly and ultimately this was to end in war. Her sorrow was increased by the Emperor William's treatment of his mother, but she remained on cordial terms with her grandson to the end of her life.

Her own domestic griefs rendered her sympathetic with the sorrows of her people, and as she grew older she more than recovered her early popularity, and was regarded with affection by the whole Empire. This affection was illustrated by the enthusiasm for her person which was shown on the occasions of her jubilees in 1887 and 1897. Her last years were clouded by the outbreak of the Boer War in South Africa (1899-1902) and by the disasters of the opening campaign, but she lived long enough to welcome Lord Roberts on his return in January 1901 after the relief of Mafeking and the annexing of the Transvaal and the Orange Free State. She died less than three weeks later and was buried at Frogmore, near Windsor Castle.

She had reigned for almost 64 years and few of her subjects could remember when she had not been their monarch. A great sense of loss was felt by the nation at her passing. Queen Victoria was a woman of robust physique, remarkable powers of memory, great force of character, deep sympathy, and sincere religious feeling. She was very tenacious of her own opinions, but understood thoroughly the position of a constitutional sovereign, and her strong common sense kept her prejudices in check.

Significant events of Victoria's reign

- 1838 – The Chartists campaign for political reforms.
- 1839 – The Anti-Corn Law League is formed.
- 1840 – The Penny Post is introduced.

  Victoria marries Albert of Saxe-Coberg-Gotha.
- 1841 – Robert Peel becomes Prime Minister.
- 1842 – China cedes Hong Kong to Britain by the Treaty of Nanking.
- 1845 – The Great Famine takes hold in Ireland.
- 1846 – The Corn Laws are repealed.
- 1848 – The year of revolutions in Europe.

  The *Communist Manifesto* is written by Karl Marx and Friedrich Engles.
- 1851 – The Great Exhibition is held in Hyde Park, London.
- 1852 – The Duke of Wellington dies.
- 1853 – Livingstone discovers Victoria Falls.
- 1854 – The Crimean War commences.
- 1857 – The Indian Mutiny.
- 1858 – Government of India is taken over by the British Crown.

- 1859 – *Origin of the Species* is written by Charles Darwin.
- 1861 – The American Civil War commences.

  Prince Albert dies.
- 1863 – The foundation of the Salvation Army.
- 1865 – The American Civil War ends.
- 1867 – The Second Reform Act doubles the electoral franchise to over two million.
- 1868 – Gladstone becomes Prime Minister.
- 1869 – The Irish Church ceases to exist with the passing of the Disestablishment Act.
- 1870 – The Education Act makes primary education compulsory.
- 1871 – Trade Unions are legalized.
- 1872 – The secret ballot is introduced for elections.
- 1876 – Victoria is created Empress of India.
- 1884 – Electoral franchise is further extended by the Third Reform Act.
- 1886 – The Irish Home Rule Bill is defeated in Parliament.
- 1887 – Victoria's Golden Jubilee year.

  The Independent Labour Party is founded.
- 1893 – The Second Irish Home Rule Bill is defeated by the House of Lords.
- 1897 – Victoria's Diamond Jubilee year.
- 1899 – The Boer War begins.

Vortigern British tribal king of Kent. Reigned *c.*450. According to the *Anglo-Saxon Chronicle* Kent was the first of the Anglo-Saxon kingdoms; founded around 450 by Jutes from Denmark and the Rhineland. 'Vortigern', the title used for an overlord, also came to be used as the name of the tribal leader who is thought to have asked mercenaries from Jutland to help him fight off attacks from northern Picts. Led by the brothers HENGEST and HORSA, the Jutes landed at Ebbsfleet, near Ramsgate, and, after driving back the Picts, turned on Vortigern and settled the area themselves.

W

Wiglaf King of Mercia. Reigned from 827 to 840. He was expelled by the powerful EGBERT of Wessex in 827 but regained the throne within a year. He is buried at Repton Monastery in Derbyshire.

Wihtred King of Kent. Reigned from 690 to 725. Ruled jointly with SUAEBHARD to 692 and married three times. A strong ruler, he successfully resisted repeated Mercian attempts to control his kingdom.

Willlam (I) the Conqueror (1027-1087) King of England. Reigned from 1066 to 1087. Born in Normandy, the illegitimate son of Robert, Duke of Normandy, by Arlotta, the daughter of a tanner of Falaise. His father having no legitimate son, William became the heir at his death, Robert of Normandy having made a pilgrimage to Jerusalem from which he did not return. William ruled Normandy with great vigour and displayed tremendous military ability. The opportunity of gaining a wider dominion presented itself on the death of his second cousin EDWARD the Confessor, king of England, whose crown he claimed by virtue of Edward's promise, made in 1051, that William would succeed him.

HAROLD had himself sworn fealty to William after falling into the hands of his rival in 1064. However, on his deathbed Edward named Harold as his successor and Harold duly accepted the crown. To enforce his claim to the throne William invaded England with a fleet of many hundreds of ships. The decisive victory at Hastings in 1066 in which Harold was killed, ensured his success.

After being crowned on Christmas Day he began establishing the administration of law and justice on a firm basis throughout England, conferred numerous grants of land on his own followers, and introduced the feudal constitution of Normandy in regard to tenure and services. At least 78 castles were built in this period. He also expelled numbers of the English Church dignitaries and replaced them with Normans. In the early years of his reign, however, William had to deal with rebellion against his rule from the Anglo-Saxons, many of whom had been dispossessed of their estates in favour of their Norman conquerors. Uprisings in the southwest (1067) and the north (1069-70) of the country were ruthlessly crushed and the defeat of the rebellion of Hereward the Wake (1070-1072) effectively ended Saxon resistance. William also invaded Scotland and forced the Scots king MALCOLM III to recognize him as overlord at Abernethy, taking his son as a hostage. Towards the end of his reign he instituted in 1085 a general survey of the landed property of the kingdom, the record of which still exists under the title of *Doomsday Book*.

In 1087 he went to war with France, where his son had encouraged a rebellion of Norman nobles. He entered the French territory, and destroyed much of the countryside, but when he burnt Mantes, his horse trod on a hot cinder and stumbled, and he was thrown forward in his saddle and received an internal injury which caused his death at the abbey of St Gervais, near Rouen. He left Normandy and Maine to his eldest son, Robert, and England to his second son, William.

Significant events of William I's reign

- 1067 – A revolt in the south west is subdued.

  Work begins on the building of the Tower of London.

- 1069 – William subdues the north of England.

- 1070 – Hereward the Wake's Saxon rebellion erupts in eastern England.

- 1072 – William invades Scotland.

- 1079 – Work begins on Winchester cathedral.

  William is victorious against his son, Robert, at Gerberoi, Normandy.

  The New Forest is made a royal hunting ground.

- 1086 – The *Domesday Book* is completed.

William (I) the Lion (1143-1214) King of Scots. Reigned from 1165 to 1214. The brother of MALCOLM IV and the grandson of DAVID I, he became king at the age of 22. His first act as king was to attempt to reclaim Northumbria, which had been taken from

Scotland by HENRY II in 1154. He mounted an expedition to this end in 1174, timing his move to exploit the strife which the English king was suffering after his murder of Thomas á Becket. However, whilst besieging Alnwick Castle the Scots were taken by surprise by an English force led by Geoffrey of Lincoln and Randulph of Glanville. William was captured and was taken to Henry II at Northampton, with his feet shackled beneath the belly of a horse. Henry II, who had that very day finished his public penance for Becket's murder, must have been soothed by the capture of the Scots king. William was imprisoned at Falaise Castle in Normandy where the following December, he was obliged to accept the terms of the Treaty of Falaise under which he was to acknowledge the sovereignty of England over Scotland including himself, his kingdom and the Scottish church.

Scotland had become a vassal kingdom. The chief Scottish castles were placed under English control and William's younger brother David, along with more than twenty of the Scottish nobility, were taken hostage to England. William was released a few months later but found on his return that in his absence unrest had broken out. The Celtic chiefs took advantage of William's imprisonment and the resentment felt by them towards the friendships of Scottish kings with their Norman neighbours turned into rebellion. The first uprisings took place in Galloway, where several nobles, who had been loyal to William and marched with him into England, now wished for

Galloway to be independent from the rest of William's kingdom. The nobles seized the royal castles, expelled the king's men and requested of Henry II that he take Galloway from William and become its overlord. Only too willing to do this, Henry sent envoys to Galloway but by the time they arrived the nobles had had a falling out. Order was not restored to Galloway for over ten tears.

The Celts of the north also rose during William's imprisonment; the men of Ross attacked Norman settlers who had been granted lands. William, after his release, travelled north to subdue his unruly subjects in 1179 and established two castles in Ross to keep order. Two years later the king was obliged to go north again, this time to subdue a rival for the throne, Donald MacWilliam, who claimed to be the great-grandson of MALCOLM III and Ingibjorg. Mac-William, who had become a powerful chief in the North, was killed at Badenoch but the rebellion took almost seven years to subdue and temporarily took Ross out of the kings control. With the death of Henry II in 1189 relations with England took a turn for the better. William was able to buy back Scotland's sovereignty for 10,000 marks, raised by taxation, on the accession of RICHARD I as the new English king was in dire need of money to fund the Third Crusade. Also, the two remaining castles under English control, Berwick and Roxburgh, were returned to Scotland. With the proclamation of Pope Celestine III in 1192 that the Kirk should be independent under the jurisdiction of Rome the independence of the

Scottish Church from Canterbury was restored. The final clause of the Treaty of Falaise was done away with on the agreement of Richard I that William should do homage to the English king only for William's English lands. The independence of Scotland had been regained but William still had designs on Northumbria which remained in English hands. He made his claim to Richard I on the English king's return from the Crusade but to no avail. William tried to buy Northumbria, Westmorland and Cumberland from Richard and made the offer of his daughter Margaret as a bride for Richard's nephew but these attempts were all in vain.

When Richard I died and was succeeded by King JOHN, William renewed his claims to the new king but John replied by beginning a fortress at the mouth of the River Tweed and shortly after invaded Scotland. William waited for him at Roxburgh Castle but negotiation took the place of battle and it was agreed that, in return for 15,000 marks and two of William's heiresses, John would not build a castle at the Tweed. William's lifelong ambition to gain Northumbria was never achieved.

Even although William was unable to realize dominion over Northumbria, his reign can be seen as successful. He regained the independence of Scotland and of the Scottish Church and, through his encouragement of the growth of the towns and the creation of many Royal Burghs, was able to improve the lives of his subjects. William is also credited with being responsible for the incorporation of the lion rampant into the royal coat of arms. William married Ermengarde de Beaumont in 1186 who bore him three daughters and one son, who was to succeed him as ALEXANDER II. He died at Stirling at the age of 72 and was buried at Arbroath Abbey which he had founded in 1178.

Significant events of William I's reign

- 1174 – William invades England but is captured and imprisoned in Normandy.

  Under the Treaty of Falaise Scotland loses its independence from England.

  Revolt breaks out in Galloway and Ross.

- 1178 – Arbroath Abbey is founded.

- 1179 – William subdues the rebels in Ross.

- 1186 – Order is restored to Galloway.

- 1189 – Henry II dies and is succeeded by Richard I.

  William buys Scotland's sovereignty back from England for 10,000 marks.

- 1192 – Pope Celestine III declares the Scottish Church to be independent under Rome.

- 1199 – Richard I of England is succeeded by King John.

William II (Rufus) (1056-1100) King of England. Reigned from 1087 to 1100. The third son of WILLIAM I and Matilda of Flanders was born in Normandy and gained the nickname 'Rufus' on account of his florid complexion. He was nominated by his father to the English succession in preference to his elder brother Robert. The Norman barons supported Robert however, and in 1088 attempted to depose William. The rebellion in Normandy was defeated by William, who secured the aid of Lanfranc, Archbishop of Canterbury, and the English nobles and Robert was given the Duchy of Normandy in place of the English crown. This was not the last revolt against his rule William would have to deal with as, in 1090, a further rising by his brother necessitated an invasion of Normandy to subdue him. Robert's departure to join the First Crusade in 1096 ensured no further trouble from that quarter.

The Scots however, proved to be difficult neighbours; an invasion of northern England by MALCOLM III of Scotland in 1091 was defeated and the Scots king was compelled to accept William as overlord. Nonetheless a further invasion was undertaken by Malcolm two years later. Again the Scots were defeated and Malcolm III was ambushed and killed, together with his eldest son Edward, at the Battle of Alnwick. Malcolm's son from his marriage to Ingibjorg, DUNCAN, who had resided in England since his being taken hostage by WILLIAM I in 1072, was dispatched north with William II's support at the head of an English army to wrest the throne from Malcolm's successor DONALD III in 1094. William's intention was for Duncan to rule Scotland as his vassal, but he only spent a few months on the throne before being killed. In 1097 William sent a second army north, this time with EDGAR, a son of Malcolm III and Margaret, who had sworn fealty to the English king, at its head. This expedition met with greater success and Edgar was installed as king.

Further warfare was conducted, this time against the Welsh whose risings against the Norman barons in the border lands resulted in an invasion of Wales being undertaken in 1098. William also encountered trouble in ecclesiastical matters, with which he dealt in a somewhat unscrupulous manner. A characteristic incident was his contention with Anselm, Archbishop of Canterbury, in 1097 regarding Church property and the sovereignty of the Pope; Church property was regarded by William as the property of the King and as such he would not allow the election of Abbots to vacant abbey's. Anselm asked for leave to receive the Pope's decision on the matter but this too was contentious as William had not officially recognised the sovereignty of any pope. At length William did recognize Pope Urban II but the quarrels between them escalated and resulted in Anselm's exile in France and the loss of all his lands.

William II met his death while chasing deer in the New Forest; killed by an arrow shot accidentally or otherwise from the bow of a French gentleman named Walter Tyrrel. The crown then passed to William's brother, HENRY I.

Significant events of William II's reign

- 1088 – Supporters of William's
  brother, Robert, rebel in Normandy.
- 1090 – William invades Normandy.
- 1093 – Malcolm III invades England.

- 1095 – Durham Cathedral is founded.

  A revolt by William's northern barons is
  put down.

- 1096 – Robert, William's brother, joins the First
  Crusade.

- 1097 – Archbishop Anselm is exiled.

- 1098 – William enters Wales to subdue a
  rebellion.

- 1099 – Jerusalem is captured by the Crusaders.

William III (William of Orange) (1650-1702) King of
England, Scotland and Ireland (respectively as
William III, II and I). Reigned from 1689 to 1702.
The son of William II of Nassau, Prince of Orange,
and Henrietta Mary Stewart, daughter of CHARLES I
of England. During his early life in Holland all power
was in the hands of the grand pensionary John De
Witt, but when France and England in 1672 declared
war against the Netherlands, there was a popular revolt, in which Cornelius and John De Witt were murdered, while William was declared Captain-General,
Grand-Admiral, and Stadtholder of the United Provinces. In the campaign which followed he opened the
sluices in the dykes and flooded the country around
Amsterdam forcing the French to retreat, while peace
was soon made with England. In subsequent campaigns
he lost the battles of Seneffe (1674) and St Omer (1677),
but was still able to keep the enemy in check.

In 1677 he was married to MARY, daughter of the
Duke of York, later JAMES II of England, and the
Peace of Nijmegen followed in 1678. For some years

subsequent to this the policy of William was directed to curbing the power of Louis XIV, and to this end he brought about the League of Augsburg in 1686. As his wife was heir presumptive to the English throne, he had kept close watch upon the policy of his father-in-law, James II, and in 1688 he issued a declaration recapitulating the unconstitutional acts of the English king, and promising to secure a free Parliament to the people. He was invited over to England by seven of the leading statesmen, who feared that James II's newly born son would be brought up as a Catholic. Arrivng suddenly at Torbay (with a fleet of 500 ships, and with 14,000 troops) the greater part of the nobility declared in his favour. James fled with his family to France and William made his entry into London. The throne was now declared vacant and, upon William and Mary's acceptance of the Declaration of Rights, which defined the limits of regal power and fixed the succession, barring Catholics from the throne, William and Mary were proclaimed joint monarchs of England and Scotland.

The 'Glorious Revolution' was virtually complete in England but the situation in Scotland was to take a little longer to resolve. A few months after James II's flight, John Graham of Claverhouse, the Viscount Dundee, raised the royalist standard and defeated an English army at Killiecrankie. Dundee was killed in the battle and without his leadership the rebellion's momentum was lost. A further battle took place in August the same year at Dunkeld but the outcome was indecisive, although both claimed victory. The

rising in Scotland rumbled on for a further ten
months until the remaining rebels were overcome at
Cromdale in early 1690. However an incident two
years later was to prove a boon for Jacobite propa-
gandists. John Dalrymple, Master of Stair and
William III's principal minister in Scotland, was
placed in charge of effecting the royal decree that
each Highland chief must abandon their loyalty to
the deposed king and swear an oath of loyalty to their
new king. The deadline for taking this oath was set
for the 1st of January 1692 and most of the clan
chiefs did as asked. MacIan of the Clan MacDonald
was late in giving his oath, having first travelled mis-
takenly to Fort William. The oath was eventually
given but a troop of soldiers, acting on the orders of
Dalrymple, nevertheless set about the slaughter of
the 200 families of the Clan MacDonald who were
encamped at Glencoe. The government inquiry
which followed in 1695 was indecisive, but the Scottish Parliament decided, at length, that Dalrymple
was responsible and he was subsequently dismissed.
However, by now attention in Scotland had shifted to
consideration of the ill-fated Darien Scheme. Scotland, excluded from any part of the wealth generated
in England from its trade with its far-flung colonies,
decided to establish a colony of its own. An Act
passed in 1693 for the purpose of encouraging foreign trade, together with the setting up of the Company of Scotland, with powers granted by Parliament
to found new colonies, laid the foundations of the
scheme. The site for the proposed colony lay in

Spanish territory and Spain did not approve of the founding of a 'New Caledonia' on its property; in addition, the area became a fever-infested swamp in the summer. The two expeditions to Darien were catastrophic. Fever claimed the lives of many of the colonists and the English possessions in the West Indies refused supplies to the stricken colony which was then closed down by Spanish troops. It was a financial disaster which was widely felt and certainly did nothing to improve Anglo-Scottish relations.

In Ireland the accession of William III was no less troubled than it had been in Scotland. In 1689 the Catholics rose up against William's rule in support of James II and some 30,000 or more Protestants fled to take refuge in Londonderry. James II landed with a small number of French troops sent by Louis XIV and laid siege to the city. Relief came more than 100 days later from an English fleet. James and his mostly Irish army moved south, having failed to take Londonderry, to the River Boyne, near Drogheda. In the battle with William III's forces which ensued James II's army was crushed. James escaped to France and was not to return. William, having defeated the rebellions against his reign, attempted to allow Catholics in Ireland freedom of worship in the Treaty of Limerick (1691); however in this he was thwarted for the Protestant dominated Irish Parliament subsequently passed harsh laws which effectively made the Catholics second class citizens.

In the war with France William was less successful than he had been against his enemies at home; but although he was defeated at Steinkirk (1692) and Neerwinden (1693), Louis XIV was finally compelled to acknowledge him as king of England at the Peace of Ryswick in 1697. Friction between William and Louis XIV continued however, the final straw coming on the death of James II in 1701. Louis XIV acknowledged James's son as JAMES III of England; this showed a blatant disregard for the treaty of 1697. In addition to this, Louis banned the import of English goods to France and advised Philip V of Spain to do likewise.

England, Holland, and the Austrian Empire had already combined against Louis XIV in the Grand Alliance of 1701 and the War of the Spanish Succession, to prevent the union of the Spanish and French crowns, was just on the point of commencing when William died from the effects of a fall from his horse. A hard-working and able monarch, William III was nevertheless unpopular; probably due to his reserved nature, his poor understanding of the English language and his undisguised preference for his beloved Holland. He was succeeded by his sister-in-law, ANNE.

Significant events of William III's reign

- 1689 – The Bill of Rights is passed.

  Jacobites defeat government forces at Killiecrankie.

  James II lays siege to Londonderry.

- 1690 – The Jacobites are defeated at Cromdale.

  James II is defeated at the Battle of the Boyne.

- 1691 – The Treaty of Limerick allows freedom of worship for Irish Catholics.

  War with France breaks out.

- 1692 – The Massacre of Glencoe.

- 1694 – Queen Mary dies.

- 1697 – The French war is ended by the Peace of Ryswick.

- 1698 – The Darien Scheme is launched.

- 1701 – The Act of Settlement establishes Protestant Hanoverian succession.

  The exiled James II dies.

  The War of the Spanish Succession begins.

William IV (1765-1837) King of the United Kingdom of Great Britain and Ireland. The third son of GEORGE III and Charlotte of Mecklenburg-Strelitz. He served in the navy, rising successively to all the grades of naval command, until in 1801 he was made Admiral of the Fleet. In 1789 he had received the title of Duke of Clarence and, after retiring from the Navy in 1790, settled down with the actress Dorothea Jordan. He lived a happily domestic life with his mistress, who bore him ten children, though financial needs neccessitated her frequent returns to the stage. However, in 1811, with the worsening condition of George III and uncertainty over the succession, William left Mrs Jordan and searched for a wife; at length marrying Adelaide of Saxe-Meningen in 1818.

At the age of 64 he succeeded his brother, GEORGE IV,

as king, amid much concern over his fitness for the crown; he was given to strong language, was well-known for his forthright opinions, and his lack of tact had earned him the nickname 'Silly Billy'. However, his blunt speech and lack of pretence soon won him the affection of the public. He was king during a period of some considerable political upheaval, a few of the great events which render his reign memorable being the passage of the Reform Act, the abolition of slavery in the colonies, and the reform of the Poor Laws. He was the last sovereign to try to chose his prime minister regardless of parliamentary support; replacing Melbourne with Peel in 1834. He died at Windsor Castle after a reign of only seven years. His two daughters by Adelaide of Saxe-Meningen had died in infancy, and, leaving no other legitimate heir, he was succeeded by his niece Victoria.

Significant events of William IV's reign

- 1830 – The first passenger steam railways open.

- 1831 – Old London Bridge is demolished.

- 1832 – The First Reform Act greatly increases the electoral franchise.

- 1833 – The Factory Act forbids the employment of children below the age of nine.

    Slavery in British colonies is abolished.

- 1834 – The Tolpuddle Martyrs are transported.

    Workhouses are introduced under the Poor Law.

- 1837 – Charles Dickens writes *Oliver Twist*.

Wuffa (d.*c*.578) King of East Anglia. Reigned from 571 to *c*.578. Considered to be the first king of the East Angles. The term 'Wuffings' was applied to all following kings up to the time when the kingdom was merged with Mercia around 800. He was succeeded by his son, TYTILA.

Wulfhere (d.675) King of Mercia. Reigned from 657 to 675. A younger brother of PEADA, he led the Mercian campaign to overthrow Northumbrian hegemony and invaded Wessex in 674. He gave the Isle of Wight to King ETHELWALH of Sussex.